P9-CBU-005

And Suddenly It's Evening

And Suddenly It's Evening

A FRAGMENT OF LIFE

Mabel Barbee Lee

Doubleday & Company, Inc., Garden City, New York, 1963

For

Barbara
my beloved daughter

and

Ishbel
our friend all the way

Each alone on the heart of the earth,
impaled upon a ray of sun:
and suddenly it's evening.

Salvatore Quasimodo

INTRODUCTION

by Lowell Thomas

I wonder what the distance is from Cripple Creek to Radcliffe? The rough-and-tumble mining camp is certainly farther from the college for young ladies than mere geography would indicate. The old-time prospectors who flocked to the gold fields beyond Pike's Peak were about as handy with the books as any coed would be swinging a pick at the bottom of the Independence or the Golden Cycle. While the girls who interested the Harvard men were studying Elizabethan literature, we boys of Cripple Creek were picking up an Elizabethan vocabulary among the miners, the drifters, and the saloonkeepers.

But if you want to know the connection between the Colorado camp and the Massachusetts college in personal terms, I can tell you the answer. Her name is Mabel Barbee Lee.

In 1958 I had the privilege of introducing Mabel Barbee Lee to the reading public. I wrote the Foreword to her dramatic story of a dramatic place and time: *Cripple Creek Days*. Hers was a labor of love, and so was mine. How familiar it all seemed as Mabel's brilliant account jogged my memory of people and events dating from the time around the turn of the century when she arrived, fresh, beautiful, and enthusiastic, to teach the wayward boys of Victor, Colorado, myself included, in the red-brick high school just a block down Victor Avenue from the red-light district.

When my schooldays were over, our paths diverged. I was a rolling stone, wandering from place to place around the planet as my fancy took me. And the lovely young schoolmarm who had inspired me, or at least tried to—what of her? Well, Mabel and I have spent wonderful moments together reminiscing about the old days in Cripple Creek, and I've heard her speak of her marriage, and her widowhood, and her problem of raising a daughter by herself (no mean feat back when women had just got the vote and it was considered unladylike to work). But I never realized how colorful the later chapters of her biography were until I received the proofs of this autobiography.

Although Mabel had received her B.A. degree at Colorado College, one still marvels at the wisdom that brought her an offer to return to her alma mater—and as publicity director, no less! Someone with sense had been reading her articles in magazines and newspapers. The job was supposed to be temporary, but I could have told the trustees that they would not be able to let Mabel go. Presto! We find her Dean of Women at Colorado College, headed into the Roaring Twenties and guiding some rather unruly coeds who acted like flappers, went with boyfriends in raccoon coats, and knew all about bathtub gin.

At that time, anyone who made a noise in the West was sure to be enticed East. Radcliffe heard about Mabel Barbee Lee of Colorado, and soon she was ruling the prim halls of ivy, if not with an iron rod, at least with a firm hand. It must have been quite an experience for those sedate Eastern misses who sat at the feet of their housemistress and heard all about Shakespeare and Hawthorne—and the redhead known as "the Boilermaker" in Cripple Creek's tenderloin.

I could go on and on, but that would be like the toastmaster outtalking the speaker of the evening. What I really want to say is this. I hope that you read *Cripple Creek Days*. I believe that you will enjoy the sequel that you hold in your hand: *And Suddenly It's Evening*. I know that you will admire the author, my old friend, Mabel Barbee Lee.

Foreword

In The Way of All Flesh written almost a hundred years ago, Samuel Butler said: "Every man's work whether it be literature or music or pictures or architecture or anything else, is always a portrait of himself and the more he tries to conceal himself the more clearly will his character appear in spite of him. I may very likely be condemning myself all the time that I am writing this book for I know that whether I like it or not, I am portraying myself more surely than I am portraying any of the characters whom I may set before the reader. I'm sorry it is so but I can not help it. . . ."

Since I am not known to be photogenic—a word that came into use long after Butler's day—either in face or figure, this sentiment must apply to me, especially the last apologetic sentence. And I feel moved to make some of my own confessions.

My intention was not to write about colleges. That has been done again and again by scholars who speak with authority. They happened to form the setting for my career. A different kind of drama would have been enacted, doubtless, if I had ever become a professional author, or a secretary, or a clerk in a department store. But that was the way it was for me. I have avoided faculty personalities except where necessary to the story and, with the exception of Bennington College, I tried to avoid critical academic controversies which seemed to have no place in the book.

The names of students are generally fictitious, and the problems in which they were involved, while based on facts, were sometimes scrambled. Neither the students nor the problems were peculiar to any one institution but were common phenomena of the times. The girl, Penny, for whom I developed great affection and sympathy, was a complete fabrication, "a lobe of my brain," to paraphrase Stuart Sherman, "which I took out and dressed up somewhat like a modern flapper." (In the same vein, I may add that she turned out surprisingly well in spite of all of Jessie's dire predictions. The last I heard, some years ago, she was getting ready to send the eldest of her five daughters to "dear old C.C. where she will have the careful supervision of a resident Dean of Women. She's the only one of my girls," the letter went on to say, "that I've never felt close to, and I don't understand. . . .")

A half century hence, some astute sociologist will write another history of the emancipation of woman and he will point out that her most tragic era started after the First World War, in the 1920s, when the possibility of marriage became remote and she was catapulted from the home into occupations for which she was unprepared by temperament, training, or experience. That she succeeded in making the adjustment, often with distinction, is one of the miracles of the age.

I do not fall into that happy category. My only assets were an enjoyment of people, especially the young. My failures have been many and my triumphs few and far apart but I never lost a certain excitement about life and an urge for learning. Above all, I was rich in friends. Never was there a crisis when I could not find a hand reaching out to give me a lift, or a word of encouragement. Their faces are dimming but friends of the troubled years of my early widowhood, such as Mrs. Adelaide

C. Lumgair, will never be forgotten. Of more recent times, I
wish to express my heartfelt thanks to Mrs. George Belsey of
Santa Barbara, who took time out of her busy days to type my
manuscript. Only another writer can fully appreciate such an
act of friendship. And to you, Wolcott and Marka Stewart, go
my affection and abiding gratefulness for your many kindnesses
and unfailing interest and inspiration.

From time to time, short articles of mine have appeared in
various periodicals. The most recent have been in the *Empire*
magazine of the Denver *Post* and the Bennington College
Alumnae Quarterly, from which I have borrowed freely. I also
found most fascinating a story, "Some Recollections of the Beginnings of Bennington College," written by Edith van Ben-
thuysen McCullough (Mrs. Hall Park McCullough) and published in the *Bennington College Bulletin,* in June 1957.
Hudson Strode's *Sweden—Model for a World* refreshed my recollections of that delightful country. Barbara Jones' authoritative
little book, *Bennington College,* published by Harper & Bros.,
would prove of great interest to anyone desiring more information than I have been able to include about this experiment in
modern education. Certain books became turning points in my
career, such as James Harvey Robinson's *The Mind in the Making,* from which I have quoted briefly; Walter Lippmann's *A
Preface to Morals;* Theodore Dreiser's *An American Tragedy;*
and Mary P. Follet's *Creative Experience.*

I should like to express my obligation to Mr. Brainerd Mears
and Mr. Fred Mears of Williamstown, Massachusetts, brothers
of the late Ruth Mears Sherman, for their permission to quote
parts of the letters to me published in *Stuart Pratt Sherman—
His Life and Letters,* edited by Jacob Zeitlin and Homer Wood-
bridge for Holt, Rinehart & Winston, Inc. These acknowledg-
ments would not be complete without mention of the help
given me at crucial points by Mr. Robert Gates and his compe-

tent staff in the reference department of the Santa Barbara Library.

Finally, I shall be forever indebted to Signor Salvatore Quasimodo, the distinguished poet and Nobel Laureate in Literature for 1959, and to his publisher, l'Editeur Arnoldo Monadori de Milano for granting me the privilege of quoting the beautiful poem, *And Suddenly It's Evening*, on the flyleaf and using the title for my book.

Mabel Barbee Lee

And Suddenly It's Evening

PART I

THE TRANSITION

1

It was a freshman whom I shall call Penny,
or perhaps it was Penny's mother, who initiated me into what
later became known as the "Roaring Twenties." I had arrived in September 1922 to take over the post as Dean of
Women at Colorado College, in Colorado Springs. The campus
was not altogether strange to me. I had been a student there,
some sixteen years before, but most of my life since then had
been spent as the wife of a mining engineer, in camps far removed from the chaste atmosphere of the college world. News
seldom came except in letters seeking various contributions or
from bits of gossip brought by some visiting classmate.

The appointment had followed an incredible chain of circumstances. Howe, my husband, died in 1918, leaving me with
very little money and a six-year-old daughter, Barbara, to support. We were in Denver at the time and, fortunately, Howe's
family took us in until I could find work. They were disheartening days. Two years of teaching in one of the Cripple Creek
high schools before my marriage was my only experience in
earning a living. But a whole decade had passed and I was out
of touch with newer educational practices, and there was
neither time nor money for further, necessary study.

My only other asset seemed to be a flair for writing. A few
western magazines and newspapers had published several of

my stories and articles and, with Howe's encouragement, I dreamed of becoming a successful author someday. It was on this slender offering that I secured a position as publicity secretary of the West Central Field of the Young Women's Christian Association. The modest salary was not enough to assure independence, and the future was uncertain. The office would be closed when the war fund which had underwritten it was spent, possibly in two or three years. Meanwhile, however, I would be getting valuable training which might lead to something permanent elsewhere. My spirits soared. The longed-for home with Barbara seemed to be in sight!

But as the deadline neared and the war money dwindled and still nothing substantial had developed, I began to fear the worst. Soon I would be back facing the same dilemmas and wondering where to turn next. It began to look as if I would never be able to make it on my own and I imagined that Howe's family had about reached the same conclusion. Barbara was not an easy child to manage and caused considerable worry for her aging grandmother. Out of desperation I took a night course in shorthand and typing, which was considered an entering wedge for all sorts of vocations. But I had no aptitude for such work. My hands were fumbling and awkward and my patience too limited. Courage and hope seemed to have struck rock bottom.

Then, out of the blue one day, a letter came from Dr. C. A. Duniway, the new president of Colorado College, saying that the Board of Trustees planned to embark on an endowment campaign and he wondered if I would be interested in taking charge of the publicity, especially in connection with the alumni. "We are looking for someone, preferably a graduate of the college," he wrote, "who has had experience in public relations and you have been highly recommended. The salary would be $300.00 a month and expenses. Please let me hear from you at your earliest convenience. . . ."

My first impulse was to write an immediate acceptance, but the few friends with whom I talked showed less enthusiasm. They reminded me that the college had been torn by serious dissensions for several years. The former, long-time president had retired under a cloud of rumor and gossip and some of the best teachers had left. The student body was decreasing alarmingly and many of the dormitory rooms stood empty. The alumni, bitterest and most articulate of all, berated the Board of Trustees and their new presidential appointment. "It is the worst time imaginable," my friends declared, "to undertake an endowment campaign. In a few months," they warned, "you may find yourself high and dry, out of a job and with nowhere to go."

But I saw no alternative. Barbara would be ten shortly, and with a liberal salary I could send her to a good boarding school for little girls. This would free me for a year, at least, for the difficult task of getting organized. If all went well, something better might develop which would enable me to rent a small house in town and send for her.

I had scarcely unpacked my trunk when misgivings began to assail me. The roar of battle was growing louder. My fellow alumni seemed unimpressed by me and my appeals for their co-operation. In fact, they served only to sharpen the determination to get rid of the unpopular president. Now I, too, was in the camp of the enemy and apparently regarded as a turncoat, a traitor to the Cause. They proceeded to initiate their own drive and urged prospective donors not to contribute funds so long as the present administration was in power. Parents were advised to send their sons and daughters to other institutions. The rift within the faculty had widened, with more instructors leaving. But the president, whom I had come to respect and trust, stated emphatically that he had no intention of resigning under fire.

Finally, the Board of Trustees announced the postponement of the endowment campaign. And I found myself, just as my friends had predicted, with only a summer's advanced salary between me and disaster. Then, unexpectedly, the Dean of Women let it be known that she had been appointed headmistress of a private school for girls in the East. On her recommendation, the harrried president offered me her position, starting with the fall semester. I debated the matter several days before coming to a decision. It meant living "in residence" in Bemis Hall, the largest of the women's dormitories, but Deans of Women were not supposed to be widows and mothers and no provision had been made for a child. I was assured, however, that there would be a place for Barbara in the guest room across the hall from the Dean's quarters.

The idea of becoming a Dean of Women and spending my life in a world of females had no attraction for me. In truth, the offer had dismayed me as much as it astounded the watchful alumni. "This is the last straw!" their raised eyebrows seemed to say. "What can that president mean by making such a ridiculous selection? How can a woman whose childhood had been shaped by the crude influences of a mining camp like Cripple Creek ever hope to maintain the social and cultural standards established by Miss Ruth Loomis, the first Dean of Women? And if the time was ripe to engage an alumna, why hadn't the choice gone to any one of a dozen other graduates far better qualified?" I pondered these questions myself, without finding the answers. All I knew was that by some twist of fate I was about to tackle a responsibility for which I felt completely inadequate. If I had realized that a social revolution, led by the Pennys of that generation, had already begun to turn the colleges of the land inside out, I might have picked up my child, like Topsy, and fled to some more peaceful haven.

But I was unusually naïve for having been brought up in

the middle of a gold rush. With the memory of my own student years still warm, I believed that all I had to do to succeed would be to follow the exemplary pattern of Miss Ruth Loomis, my own undergraduate Dean. She had come west from Vassar College in the late nineties to establish the position. Being a devoutly religious woman, the call must have appealed to her as a missionary venture. While the college boasted of enough girls of cultivated background to leaven the group, most of the others came from the dry-farming towns and mining camps of Colorado, with some from the scattered cattle ranches of Wyoming and New Mexico. These rugged homelands were no handicap to the boys, who often made excellent football players. But more refinement was needed for their sisters if they were to become teachers and mingle with polite society. And since their conduct was supposed to have a civilizing influence on the men students, it was important to give them a certain polish along with strict moral standards.

Miss Loomis proved to be exactly the right person for the time and place. Dignity marked her bearing, and her face had a cool, chiseled beauty ennobling to behold. Even her laughter was subdued and ladylike, and her taffeta-lined skirts swished in quiet elegance as she moved down the stairs to lead evening prayers in Ticknor Study. She knew all the requirements for proper young women, and, lest we should forget, a list of reminders was tacked on the inside of our closet doors.

Because of her superior qualities, the position became endowed with considerable prestige. Her name as patroness headed the list in cultural affairs. She stood next to the president's wife in receiving lines at receptions and "poured" at notable teas. On Thursday, her day at home, callers drove up to Ticknor Hall, where she lived, in shiny black electrics to be greeted by Jessie, the maid, and conducted to Miss Loomis' living room for a cup of tea. Students returning from class would tread softly up the stairs to their rooms in order not to disturb the Dean's guests.

But in the secret world of the undergraduates, the attitude was anything but reverent. She represented the stern disciplinarian to be outwitted, ridiculed, and made the butt of jokes. The campus males bragged about the ease with which they boosted their dates through the fire-escape windows, long after Jessie had locked the dormitory doors at ten o'clock. Often, the girls, resentful of restrictions and wanting approval of the boys, poked fun at the dean's admonitions and imitated her eastern accent.

Occasionally we gathered in each other's candle-lit rooms late at night to speculate about Miss Loomis' past. We guessed that she must be forty, at least, and wondered why a woman of her beauty and breeding had never married. "I'm sure she had lots of chances," Beth said, with a touch of envy. "Perhaps she suffered a blighted romance," put in Jean, "or maybe her true love died, and it wasn't likely that any other man noticed her after she became a Dean of Women." Marge, who was less sentimental, suspected that there may have been some terrible strain in the family, such as insanity, that had led her to forego marriage.

For whatever reason, Miss Loomis' spinsterhood remained an intriguing mystery to us. She always kept us at a respectful distance and we soon learned that prying into another's personal life was one of the first "not done" rules of good manners. We were in hearty agreement at one point, however, and asserted our opinion in no uncertain terms. Never by the weirdest stretch of the imagination could any of us see ourselves reduced to earning a living as a Dean of Women. And I, the fun-loving Cripple Creek girl, and the least apt to get within nodding distance of such a position, was the most emphatic of all.

"Heaven forbid," I exclaimed, throwing up my hands in horror, "that I should ever come to such a dreadful end!"

But heaven didn't forbid, and here I was two decades later, trying to squeeze into Miss Loomis' narrow shoes, with my hapless shoulders weighted down by the cloak of her formidable office!

The Dean's quarters, a spacious living room, small bedroom, and bath, with the office just beyond, occupied the southwest corner of Bemis Hall, the newest and most imposing of the women's dormitories. An enormous plate-glass window in the living room faced the west and framed a breathtaking view of Pike's Peak and the Rampart Range. Miss Loomis herself had selected the furnishings with matchless taste. A charming Venetian scene, painted by Iwill, adorned the south wall above the fireplace and blended softly with the blue velvet draperies and rosy luster of the Persian rug. Two successive deans had dwelt there since Miss Loomis' retirement, several years before, but nothing had happened to change the studied arrangement of sofas and easy chairs; and the old-lavender fragrance of her personality still seemed to linger in the air.

An unaccountable yearning to escape swept through me as I looked around the immaculate room. I felt like a stranger trespassing on forbidden premises and sat down at the Chippendale desk to get my bearings. A Van Briggle vase of white asters stood at one side and I recalled that Jessie had always kept fresh flowers on Miss Loomis' desk. She, too, had been a heritage from my youth. I had known her since my sophomore days when she was scarcely out of her teens and just starting work as a maid in Ticknor Hall. Her cheeks were as pink as peach blossoms and the coils of her golden hair, worn in a figure eight at the back of her head, gave her slight form a certain austere dignity. How the college boys teased her with their practical jokes! She often declared it a mystery why any nice girl ever married one of them, and when it happened, from time to time, she steadfastly refused to recognize the girl's married name.

How grateful I was to have her here now, to be relied on, and to give me a sense of continuity!

I glanced idly through the scattered leaflets in the desk drawer—a small handbook of regulations for dormitory students caught my eye. Except for a rule prohibiting smoking nothing was changed from my student days. A guilty twinge came over me. I had been familiar with all the little tricks of evasion and concealment and several times had lost my social privileges—walking home from church with Eric, slipping away for a stolen horseback ride with Elliott, a hike unchaperoned to Bruin Inn with Billy. What could I have to say to the erring girl today?

My attention was drawn to a brochure picturing glimpses of Bemis Hall. Boys and girls were chatting together, sedately, in the Commons, evidently having a wonderful time in a wholesome way. A heart-warming view showed students sitting around the fireplace in the Dean's living room, happily toasting marshmallows while their mentor smiled down at them in motherly approval. "Colorado College is fortunate," the legend read, "in having a resident Dean of Women. The door of her hospitable apartment is never closed. She is available at all times to guide and counsel the young women in her charge. Here on Sunday evenings, groups of students gather to hear her read poetry and plays, or to sing together the beautiful old hymns——"

Suddenly the sickening thought of Barbara gripped me. I could not see her anywhere in such a setting. She was a lively, heedless child who would be running in and out after school, scattering her books on chairs, flinging her coat here, her rubbers there, and spilling cookie crumbs on the blue velvet couch. I could hear her calling me up and down the corridors, slamming doors during quiet hours. It struck me like a blow that

Bemis Hall would never be a suitable home for my little girl, and in a desperate moment I buried my face in my arms on the desk.

It was Jessie's tapping on the open door that brought me back to reality. "Miss Barbee," she was saying, in a half-whisper, "I'm sorry to disturb you, but there's a lady here—she brought her daughter and wants to see you. I told her the halls wouldn't be open 'til day after tomorrow, and that you might not be in, but she——"

The caller was at Jessie's heels. She was surprisingly attractive, almost too young looking to have a grown child ready for college. Her hair was bobbed and curled in the latest fashion; and her lips were cherry red. She introduced herself, apologetically, and then called her daughter who had lagged behind in the doorway. "Penny, darling, come on in and meet the Dean of Women."

Penny darling shot her mother a resentful glance and moved slowly toward me, as if not relishing the invitation. She was plainly dressed in the manner of a girl just out of summer camp. In spite of her rudeness, something about her stirred my sympathy.

"Won't you sit down, Penny?" I said warmly. "I'm very glad to meet you——"

"I think she'd better wait for me in the Commons," the mother interrupted. "You don't mind, do you dear? I want a few minutes alone with the Dean—it won't take long."

Penny vanished without a word, as though grateful to escape. "She's shy," the mother explained, "and I don't understand it. You'd think that four years in one of the best private schools in the country would have given her some poise. But here she is, sixteen, and still has no manners!" She took a cigarette from her monogrammed silver case and tapped it on the back of her wrist. "Do you mind?" she asked, glancing around for an ash tray. "I can think better when I'm smoking."

I found a small Florentine glass bonbon dish and, without realizing it, opened one of the casement windows by the fireplace. It was doubtful if the pure air of Miss Loomis' abode had ever been sullied by the odor of tobacco. Now Penny's mother was blowing smoke rings in all directions, as if proud of the accomplishment. "It's a dreadful habit, I guess," she smiled, "and I only hope you forbid it among the girls. Penny has promised me that she won't touch a cigarette until she is twenty-one."

She moved closer to me on the couch and lowered her voice. "I'm going to talk freely with you," she began, "it's fair that you should know the situation. You see, Penny's father and I were divorced a few years ago and since then she hasn't had what you'd call a real home. It's terribly hard for a woman alone to bring up a child—especially a girl who was, to say the least, difficult. I'd like to marry again but that's not easy either. What man wants to take on a new wife with an unmanageable youngster?"

"What sort of work are you doing?" I said, assuming that only a woman who had to work would have trouble establishing a home.

"Oh, that isn't necessary," she laughed, "my ex-husband has been generous. Perhaps it would have been better for Penny if I'd had to find a job. I'm more or less on the loose, too restless to be tied down to running a house for just the two of us. I travel a lot—looking for the right man, to tell the truth, to complete my existence." She crushed out her cigarette and lit another. "Meanwhile, Penny has been in boarding school winters and in summer camps."

"Did you ever take her with you—on your trips?"

"Once, to Europe when she was fourteen. Neither of us enjoyed it. We seemed like strangers—she resented everything I said for her good." Tears welled in her eyes. "You should be thankful that you have only other people's daughters to worry about."

I was on the verge of putting her straight but something restrained me. "Just how can I be of help to Penny?" I asked, wondering why such a young girl had ever been admitted to the freshman class. But of course I realized that the college was hard-pressed for students, and perhaps she was unusually precocious.

"Could you possibly let her stay with you, here in Bemis Hall, until college opens? I know it's against the rules but she wouldn't be any bother—she's an extremely bright girl—you would soon come to love her. But I confess, I'm at the end of my rope. I'd like to close up my house and get as far away as possible, that is, if you would take her a bit early——"

I did not relish the idea of Penny as an advance responsibility, but there was no choice. After all, it would be only a day or two until the older students would arrive to welcome the incoming freshmen. Besides, I had become rather curious about Penny. She might bring me news of the life in boarding schools about which Barbara seldom wrote. I asked Jessie to make up the bed in the guest room and we had dinner together on trays in my apartment. "I hope you are going to enjoy college," I said, trying to melt the ice in her manner. "Other students will be arriving shortly and meanwhile you can get acquainted with me and your new surroundings. I don't think you'll be too lonely."

"Don't worry about me," she said, coolly, "I'm quite used to looking out for myself. My mother probably gave you an earful about me. I could tell you plenty about her, too. There's no love lost between us. In fact, I hate her——"

"That's sad. She spoke of you with affection," I said, stretching a point and wishing desperately to change the subject. "How would you like to go to a movie this evening? Corinne Griffith is playing in——"

"You listened to my mother," she said, ignoring the invitation, "and now you don't want to hear my side. She's been trying to get me out of her way ever since they split up. I love my Dad and wanted to live with him but he married somebody else not much older than me, right away and she objected to me." She gazed out the window at the dusky mountains, and her chin quivered. "So my mother finally sent me to boarding school where we wore middy blouses and flat heels and combed our hair in pigtails, and learned to curtsy to our elders." Her green eyes flashed at the recollection, and I noticed for the first time that her light brown curls were tied back with ribbon, in the manner of a very young girl. "Then it was summer camp, summer camp! I have woven enough baskets to reach from here to kingdom come. I wasn't wanted at home even for vacations. I'll never forgive her, never, never!"

"Penny!" I said sternly. "You must not speak of your mother in that way. I'm sure she tried to do what she thought best for you. Someday, perhaps, you will understand better."

She gave me a wry glance, as if she had heard these words many times before, and suddenly switched to another topic. "Do you have loads of rules here, the way they do in boarding school?"

"Naturally, there are some," I said, "otherwise we wouldn't be able to live together in peace. We have to learn to be considerate of other's rights. And sometimes the judgment of young people is unreliable."

"Rules are not for me," she said, buttering a roll. "I'm tired of toeing the mark all the time. In college, I intend to be free and live according to my own ideas."

"That might be risky at times. I don't know many adults

who can get away with it—we all conform in one way or another or else become boors and outcasts. There used to be a saying, when I was your age, that politeness—or consideration—is the oil that lubricates the wheels of society. It may sound old-fashioned to you but it still holds true."

"Now you sound exactly like a headmistress!" she said, throwing her head back and laughing. "I thought a Dean of Women would be different—just what is she for, anyhow?"

I was caught off guard and wanted to send her back to her mother on the first train. The image of Miss Loomis suddenly rose before my eyes. She would have dismissed Penny in short order, sent her to her room to ponder her impudence. But for some reason Penny's frankness beguiled me. At least she was honest and outspoken, and of course very young and inexperienced. I decided to be equally candid. "I can't answer your question offhand," I began, "I am new at the college this year and have much to learn." I was aware of having to temporize and improvise, for actually I did not know what a Dean of Women was for except to guide and counsel students and by her example——

"Example!" Penny exclaimed at my fumbling attempt to enlighten her. "How terrible—I'd rather be a warning any day!"

She had outwitted me on all points. It was clear that Penny was not going to be an easy person to live with even for a few days. I lit the fire in the grate, after she had gone, and sat thinking for a long time about Penny and her mother, about Barbara and me. Death and divorce were equally cruel. Either way, the home is broken and the mother left alone, half a woman, always seeking wholeness and seldom finding it. And the child, too, needs two parents and feels forsaken when one is lost. The urge to love is intrinsic—no human being can be happy until he loves and knows he is loved. So my thoughts ran while the coals in the grate turned to ashes, and the night watchman swinging his flashlight had made the midnight rounds.

Suddenly Jessie came padding down the hall in her bedroom slippers and stopped at my door. "I seen you were still up," she said in a stage whisper, "and I thought I'd better tell you that I can smell cigarette smoke coming from that new girl's room——"

Ironically enough I wanted to laugh at her pale face and wide eyes, and the frightened way she clutched her bathrobe around her waist, as if the world were coming to an end. "Forget it, Jessie," I said, casually, "her mother assured me that Penny had promised not to smoke until she was twenty-one. Besides, the dormitories aren't really open yet and the rules are not in force—just pretend she isn't here."

It was hard to tell whether Jessie was relieved or disappointed. "I declare," she mumbled, turning sharply to go. "I don't know what this generation is coming to. All I can say is, it's a good thing Miss Loomis ain't here—she'd die of shock!"

I could hear her muttering to herself all the way back down the corridor, and I had a suspicion that she had already decided that Miss Barbee would never make the grade.

Penny had been assigned to a room in one of the other dormitories and I saw little of her during the opening days, except when she came to meals in Bemis Hall. It was amazing how, almost overnight, she had changed in appearance. The plain, young boarding-school child had become a gaudy "flapper." Her skirts barely reached her knees and Jessie complained that when the girls danced in the corridor after dinner "Penny whirled in the Charleston until her spike heels cut holes in the freshly waxed floors." She wore her hair in enormous "buns" over the ears and I could have sworn that it was two shades lighter. The same boy seldom walked her home twice and the gossip was that she had so many fraternity pins that it kept her busy shifting them for various dates. But so far the student government rules had not got in her way, apparently, and all seemed well.

Too many other distractions besides Penny pressed in upon me to add to my turmoil. Miss Loomis' precepts vanished in futility. Her rules of conduct had become antiquated and had no meaning to the present generation. Students were in a ferment of change and struck wildly at anything and anybody that seemed to thwart them. The time had come to shake off old-fashioned traditions, they declared, and make the student body truly self-governing. Scarcely a meeting of the faculty passed without a petition from the Student Council. Compulsory chapel must go, they demanded, and more cuts should be allowed for class attendance. Then the missiles began to fly in my direction. Women students had been treated too long as irresponsible children, it was claimed, under the pretense that they were self-governing adults. Why, for instance, did the dormitory "inmates" have to go home from dances when they didn't want to, at the ridiculous hour of ten-thirty, when the town girls could stay until midnight? "What the Dean of Women must do," one petition read, "is to clean house and abolish the book of rules altogether!"

Once I had looked upon the august faculty as a sort of bulwark to lean on in times of crisis, but now I was discovering that instructors resented being bothered with the "irrelevant" problems of student conduct. "We are teachers," they asserted, "not nursemaids nor guardians of social customs." However, they cherished their power of veto and could usually be counted on to use it when least wanted.

My upbringing in a mining camp, with its spirit of tolerance for non-conformists, inclined me to sympathize with the students in their rebellion against restrictions. It went against my grain to be the warden who had to enforce them. The undergraduates, evidently sensing this, mistook it for weakness and the crusaders never lost a chance to press their advantage. But one concession only bred another; nothing satisfied them and no peace was in sight. It was only a question of how to hang on to what was best in the past and to face with wisdom whatever came in the future.

Psychologists had begun to write articles in the quietude of their libraries about how to understand human behavior. But I was in the front line of action with no time for theoretical quibbling. Cripple Creek, for instance, should have inured me to the sudden wave of profanity that polluted the everyday speech of girls. But actually I had never known a woman who cursed, at least not out loud. Now it was not unusual to hear a sweet, feminine voice giving vent to oaths that were once common only among males. One day a mild-mannered professor came to me almost in tears to report that a girl had "cursed him out" for flunking her in a mid-term test. "If it had been a boy," he said, pale with indignation, "I would have thrashed him, but all I could do to her was to order her from the room and expel her from class—I thought I'd better tell you—maybe she shouldn't be allowed to stay in college."

In my undergraduate days it had been considered bad taste to display affections in public. Nice girls were supposed to be cool toward the advances of boys until they were engaged. Only in this way could their virtue be safe from predatory males. A woman who expressed an interest in sex was almost beyond the pale, and might even be headed for a life of shame. This fiction had clung to me even through my years of marriage and widowhood. But now this three-letter word was no longer taboo. There was much talk of the "single standard," which did not mean curbing the sexual freedom of men but rather extending it for the women. New words such as "petting" and "necking" had crept into the vocabulary of students; and, more amazing still, girls often became brazen aggressors in love-making.

Privacy was obviously of no concern to them. Amorous displays frequently centered in the reception rooms and parlors of the dormitories, where habitual "neckers" sometimes staked out a favorite chair or cozy corner. Here they would spend hours wrapped in each other's arms, unmindful of the frowns of cleaning women trying to vacuum around their entwined feet, or the embarrassed glances of visiting dignitaries. My heart-to-heart talks with the worst offenders fell on indifferent ears. Appeals to good taste, personal dignity, and self-control made no visible impression. One student looked at me rather pityingly and said, "You don't understand, Dean Lee, that a girl simply has to neck if she wants dates—the fellows expect it. And what harm is there in it anyway? Only old fogies imagine the worst."

Not all of the girls resorted to such measures for snaring dates. Some of the more circumspect wrote home about the dreadful goings-on in the halls, often coloring the facts for dramatic effect. Before long, anxious parents deluged me with letters and telephone calls. They bedeviled me with other disturbing rumors floating around. It had been reported, so they wrote, that girdles were checked along with coats at the college dances, and that, because of excessive drinking among undergraduates, bouncers had displaced faculty wives as time-honored chaperons. Running down gossip and calming the fears of parents were soon among my most plaguing duties.

I was beginning to lose my own sensitivity to shock and had almost grown accustomed to the fraternity serenaders who shattered sleep late Sunday nights. What a far cry from the romantic ballad singers of yesteryear who softly strummed "I'm Longing for You" beneath the moonlit window of a college sweetheart! Now, at the toll of midnight a truck load of hula dancers, fire eaters, and blues artists was likely to descend upon the quadrangle in front of Bemis Hall and, in the flare of red lights, put on an act that rivaled the cheapest vaudeville.

But these exhibitions were tame compared with the wild celebration that took place when the football team won the season's pennant. It happened on Thanksgiving weekend—the time when Penny became the first girl—and the last—to be tossed in a blanket at the warming-up pep meeting the night before. What an unforgettable spectacle she made with her legs describing fantastic angles in the bonfire's glare, while the crowd sang,

"Another little job for the undertaker
Oh, yes, another little job——"

and Penny waved her arms and screamed merrily, as if she were
having the thrill of her life! I was conscious of all eyes shifting
from the tumbling, nondescript girl in the air to the Dean of
Women, sitting in the bleachers, as if waiting to see what would
be done about such a breach of custom. I was wondering about
it myself. Miss Loomis had not handed down a formula for
dealing with such an emergency. Fortunately for me, the coeds
themselves were outraged and rose up in self-defense against
any future high jinks of that sort. And Penny's initiation in a
literary society was delayed until she showed proper regret for
her folly. But, as usual, nothing was done about the boys who
had committed the prank; some of them were members of the
team and could not be bothered at such a crucial hour. "Besides," one faculty member said, "all this fuss would blow over
after vacation."

Crowds of alumni and other visitors, sporting coonskin coats
and waving black and gold banners, took over the town the
next morning. Bemis Hall fairly trembled with excitement when
the boxes of yellow chrysanthemum corsages began to arrive.
Hours before the kickoff, people started pouring onto the
bleachers of Washburn Field. A chilly breeze was blowing down
from Pike's Peak's first snowcap. It was a day to wrap steamer
rugs around one's knees and ankles, a time to clap hands and
stomp feet to keep warm while cheering the Tigers on to victory.

But, in spite of the festive air, anxiety gripped me all through
the game. Unconsciously I prayed for the home team's defeat.
The hubbub had been upsetting enough when some small, out-
of-state college was routed. What would happen if the Tigers
should win the Conference championship! The thought sent

shivers down my spine. If the alumni lived up to their reputation of flaunting the Volstead Act, they would be well supplied with hip flasks, and, as in the past, the noisy celebration would be focused on the women's quadrangle. But luck was with the Black and Gold, and when Bob McIlvaine kicked the final goal for a smashing victory I shut my eyes in foreboding.

I decided that it would be wiser for me not to attend the all-college dance in the gymnasium that night, but to remain on duty at Bemis Hall. Jessie locked the front doors, as usual, at ten o'clock and turned out the lights in the Commons and main corridors. I went to the cloak room to check the sign-out list. Apparently everyone had gone to the party. Some, like Penny, had an over-supply of dates, while others trouped together looking their prettiest and hoping to pick up a beau, at least for the walk home. I had sat with these manless girls often, as chaperon, and wondered why the boys shied away from them. They were every bit as attractive, in my opinion, as those who never missed a dance. Frequently I tried to break up the cluster of stags near the door, as if ready for quick escape, and beguile some of them into waltzing or one-stepping with a few of the wallflowers. But they would scatter in sudden alarm, as if I were about to turn the fire hose on them.

Soon they would drift back cautiously and resume their detached places at the door. Occasionally one would cut in on a cute little flirt, already swamped with partners. But it was a baffling mystery to me why the quiet, less showy, and often more intelligent type never appealed to the stag's taste. Once I even questioned Jimmie, a Bemis Hall regular, about it. "A fellow might get stuck with a dud," he said, "and go back to the frat house feeling like a fall guy. Besides, it's more fun to break in—choose the pick of the crop for a whirl—and then you can always go home when you get bored." But the wallflowers

were invariably good sports and came back to the halls singing
their theme song:

> *"Oh, I must go to the all-college dance*
> *Alone, tee-hee, alone*
> *And sit by myself with the chaperon*
> *Alone, tee-hee, alone.*
> *"But if some lad should smile at me*
> *I'd look at him and giggle with glee*
> *Possibly then I would not be*
> *Alone, tee-hee, alone!"*

What yearning hearts! What happy warriors! Out in full force
on this memorable night!

The faculty had noted the occasion by extending the closing
hour to twelve-thirty. Dormitory girls were expected to sign in
twenty minutes later, giving ample time to stroll the long way
home, with a few lingering good-bys at the door. The zero hour
was drawing near and I sat waiting in the shadows by a casement window in the Commons. Footsteps passed slowly along
the terrace and I drew back, thinking that it might be the
peeper who had been bothering the dormitories lately. It was
only the night watchman. He had been on the job since the
beginning of time, it seemed, and was so feeble that his knees
wobbled as he walked. A rickety prop on which to lean in case
of need! I pushed open the window and sniffed the frosty air.
Snatches of the latest hit, "Runnin' Wild," floated over from
the gymnasium. Only a little while longer, I sighed gratefully,
and I'd hear their laggard feet coming down the gravel path.
It had been a long day of fun and excitement for the students
and there would probably be no further celebration.

But hardly had the last girl signed in when there was a distant boom like an explosion, and voices shouting and yelling
from somewhere beyond the railroad tracks. My heart pounded.

Could it be the preliminaries to a shirttail parade? Upstairs, students began running through the corridors, slamming doors and shrieking. Suddenly the whole building seemed to shake in frenzy as the hullabaloo grew closer. Now the crazy, jubilant mob was goose-stepping down the hill and around the green in front of Bemis Hall. Jessie and I watched them from the Commons. Hundreds of men were milling about, dressed in their nightshirts and underwear. Their torchlights flashed on the yellowed maple trees and up to the window ledges of the hall where girls had begun to sing and clap as the paraders started snake dancing. All at once, out of the din a shrill, feminine voice called, "Come in—come on in—we dare you to come in to Bemis!"

"This is the worst I ever seen," Jessie said nervously. "They'll break down the door, sure as anything. You want that I should call the police?"

"No, not yet—I think we can manage——"

A youth whom I recognized as Jimmie rushed up the terrace steps and was pounding on the door, demanding that it be opened. I had to think fast; there was no telling what might happen, once that crowd got inside the house. Seeing no alternative, I flung open the door, prepared to face the worst, determined that not one of them should step over the threshold. Jimmie evidently didn't expect such an immediate response and for a moment he stammered like a small boy caught stealing cookies.

"The fellows—they want to come in," he said, with a show of bluff, "they want to dance in the Commons with the girls——"

How comical he looked in his red union suit and nightcap, with a "Keep Off the Grass" sign balancing on his shoulder! My fears vanished, oddly, and I had to smile in spite of the seriousness of the situation. "At *this* hour?" I said incredulously. "It is well after one o'clock."

"We want to dance, we want to dance," chorused the gang pushing against him. "Don't let 'er kid you, Jimmie! Come on, fellas, let's raid the Dean's beanery!"

"Cut it out," Jimmie commanded, as two of them tried to brush past me. "Hold your horses," giving them another shove back, "I'm handling this——" Then he turned to me and said, "See? They won't wait, Dean, and the sooner you give in the less trouble there'll be."

"But you couldn't possibly crowd into the Commons," I parried, sparring for time.

"We'd like a tight squeeze," someone yelled.

"She's pullin' your leg, Jim!" another cried.

Roars of approval rang out. They meant business; some kind of compromise would have to be made. As the shouting grew louder and more threatening, and Jessie tugged behind me insisting that I send for the police, I became strangely calm. An idea had struck me, so startling and bold that for an instant I faltered——

"She's stringin' us along," a voice goaded, "let's give the outfit the bum's rush—come on, heave ho!"

"Listen to me, Jimmie," I said, ignoring the others, "don't let these crazy boys do something they'll regret. Under no circumstances will I permit one of you to enter Bemis Hall. I have a suggestion instead and you can take it or leave it. In view of the Tigers' victory, I'll let the girls come out and dance with you all on the lawn, but——"

"Did you hear that, gang?" he couldn't wait until I had finished. "She's letting the girls out—we're going to dance in the quad!"

Such a thing had never been done before; the boys were stunned.

"On one condition," I went on, "the celebration must end promptly at two-thirty. Is that understood?"

"It's a deal," Jimmie said, "give my word—shake!"

The old piano was carried out and, in no time, wide-eyed girls streamed from the halls singing,

> *"Oh, you cannot twist the Tiger's tail*
> *You'd better not try, you'll surely fail——"*

and soon they were kicking and twisting in the Charleston. And now there were no wallflowers shivering close to the Dean of Women! Everybody was dancing. The harvest moon hung high over Cutler's Tower and seemed to grin broadly at the unfamiliar spectacle down below. As it neared two-thirty, the throng broke into

> *"Hail, hail, the gang's all here*
> *What the* hell *do we care*
> *What the* hell *do we care*
> *What the* hell *do we care now——"*

It was a lusty air. We had sung it back in 1906, substituting "what the what," or "what the heck" for the forbidden word, "hell." Unconsciously I was humming along, enjoying the exhilaration of old memories when I happened to see the young reporter from the *Gazette* mingling with the group, not far away.

My heart stood still! I had come to fear publicity as a many-tongued monster that fed on scandal and sensationalism. The college had already suffered enough from the wrong kind; it was particularly vulnerable because of long and bitter feuds. I glanced anxiously at the president's house not far beyond. It was dark; he and his family were spending the holidays in San Francisco. What an unwitting thing I had done in his absence! I had added fuel to the fires by allowing the girls in my care to dance with scantily dressed men, at the ungodly hour of two-thirty Sunday morning! The *Gazette's* headlines grimaced at me like ugly gnomes: DEAN OF WOMEN SANCTIONS SUNDAY MORNING BRAWL; CITIZENS UP IN ARMS DEMANDING DEAN'S RESIGNATION; BOARD OF TRUSTEES TO INVESTIGATE!

The reporter came toward me, his hands thrust in his overcoat pockets. "I'm Chuck," he said, smiling rather fiendishly it seemed, "from the *Gazette*. You must be Dean Lee—I don't think I've had the pleasure of meeting you before. Glad to see that you don't stand by the old prison rules. In my day at CC, dynamite couldn't have blasted the doors open after ten o'clock."

"Oh—so you are an alumnus——"

"Not quite—the tail end of the war caught me and I never graduated, had to go to work afterward." He lit a match and glanced at his wrist watch. "Guess the fireworks are about shot —not as exciting as I expected. Understood that the boys were all set to invade Bemis Hall and make off with one of the gals. Would have been a great story, big headlines all over the country. Except for the time of night, and it being Sunday," he added in a tone of disappointment, "it won't rate more than a mention in City Briefs. Well, so long," he added, starting to go, "we'll probably be meeting again someday."

Only a short item telling of the weekend dance in the gymnasium, marked by the return of many alumni, appeared in next day's *Gazette*. The reputation of Colorado College remained unsullied, for a while at least, and it was said that the Dean of Women had moved up a notch in student popularity. But not so with the Ministerial Alliance. The church people of the community lost no time in bringing the "disgraceful affair" to the attention of their pastors and urged investigation.

III

The Ministerial Alliance, a powerful force in
the town, acted promptly and invited the Dean of Men and me
to attend its next monthly meeting. I dreaded the encounter
and felt guilty of every crime and misdemeanor that had ever
stained the fair name of the college. I was ready, at the first
whack of the gavel, to rise up, confess everything, and hand in
my resignation. The Dean of Men was also a professor of education and, like his colleagues, showed more concern over the
students' poor scholarship than with their wanton doings outside of class. But he was a sincere, regular church attendant and
a man of quick wit. Fortunately he was the first to be questioned.

It had been reported, the chairman began, skirting the
Thanksgiving incident, that there was considerable drinking
among the students, and that it had become necessary at recent
football games to call on the police to patrol the bleachers for
drunkenness and to confiscate liquor brought in by alumni.
Could the Dean of Men throw any light on these conditions?

The Dean answered frankly, and with tongue in cheek. It
was his opinion, he said, that Prohibition had done more harm
than good. Furthermore, it had bred disrespect, especially among
young people, for all law and order. A large measure of the
blame fell upon parents who, too often, set a bad example for

their children. "We discipline the students," he went on, "whenever we can get evidence of their drinking, but it is an extremely difficult problem—as you gentlemen may understand. I have heard from reliable sources that there is a great deal of drinking among your parishioners. Some of them, it is said, even make the bathtub gin that their sons bring to the games in hip flasks. Perhaps we should work together in trying to find a solution, for, after all, many of your worshipers are parents of our undergraduates. The Dean of Women and I would appreciate your suggestions."

The discussion that followed was polite and ineffectual. No mention was made of the championship celebration on Thanksgiving weekend. The hackneyed phrases sounded flimsy and irrelevant, and the tendency was to point the finger, trying to find someone else to blame. I had the feeling that some of the ministers were wondering how they ever happened to bring up the subject and wanted to bow out as gracefully as possible. They seemed more subdued and thoughtful than when the meeting opened.

Even so, I trembled like a freshman of the early days when the chairman next turned his attention to me. He spoke in a kindly voice of my newness to the present campus and wished me well. "I do not need to remind you, as an alumna of the college, of the Christian ideals and traditions in which it was conceived. Now, as never before, those entrusted with the guidance and counseling of the students must hold fast to the time-tested purposes of the founders." He looked around at the faces of his associates and asked for questions.

A tall, thin clergyman raised his hand and stood up.

"I have been informed, Dean Lee," he drawled in a fatherly manner, "that there is talk of discontinuing the tradition of holding evening prayers in Bemis Hall—a custom almost as old as the college itself, introduced, I believe, by its first consecrated Dean of Women, Miss Ruth Loomis." He took a sip of water and cleared his throat. "I would like to know if there is any truth in this report." Again he cleared his throat, as if sharing my own nervousness. "Do you suppose this loss of religious interest has any bearing on the dwindling church attendance of the young women living in the dormitories, away from home influence?"

After reassuring him about the continuance of evening prayers, although they were somewhat anemic because of lack of support, I confused the issue of church attendance—a criticism which I honestly couldn't meet. I myself was guilty in that respect, never having acquired the habit because houses of worship were scarce in the mining camps where I lived. Instead, I dwelt on the fine character of the women students. In general, I declared feelingly, they were eager for an education and were looking forward to becoming intelligent mothers and good companions to their husbands. I was conscious of the rapt attention of the ministers and was carried along by the exhilaration of the moment to sing further praises of the model young women at Colorado College.

All of a sudden, my paean came to an abrupt end and my mind went blank. In a far corner of the room, I had caught sight of Chuck, the ubiquitous reporter from the *Gazette*. Panic seized me for a moment. What had I said that could be played up in headlines detrimental to the college? Nothing, absolutely nothing that the most proper citizen could criticize. Never had I been more sure of the dignity and good taste of my remarks. They were in the true Loomis vein. I almost saw her nodding approval.

But this time Chuck's nose for news had pounced on a front-

page story that made copy for papers as far away as Chicago.
The bold, black caption read,

> Dean of Women Tells Ministers
> College Flappers Hope to be
> Hubby's Pal!

IV

The ordeal with the ministers had been a sobering experience. I brooded over it a great deal, taking stock of my shortcomings. It struck me as I lay sleepless one night that, so far, I had been improvising solutions from crisis to crisis and mistaking a small measure of popularity for success. Even the clergymen to whom parents and educators turned for guidance had to fall back on the maxims and moralizations of the past. Their words no longer carried the power of authority.

All the while the young clamored for "self-expression," without knowing what kind of self to express. They cried for more and more freedom without knowing how to use it. Adults seemed equally confused and beat about vainly seeking answers, trying to understand the change that had come over the younger generation. Some gave up and, like their sons and daughters, joined the fight against conformity and restraint. One thing was clear to me, as I tossed in the dark—there was no turning back. However much the preachers exhorted and the deans belabored and punished, the inevitable sweep of tomorrow was upon us, to be faced with whatever wisdom we could muster.

I switched on the light and reached for the new book on my bedside table. It was called *The Mind in the Making*,[1] by James

[1] Harper & Bros., New York, 1921.

Harvey Robinson, a heavy-sounding volume that promised to put me to sleep. But as I fingered through the preface an excerpt from Walter Lippmann's *Drift and Mastery*[2] caught my attention. I read on, spellbound; the words seemed to have been written for me:

"Never before have we had to rely so completely on ourselves," Lippmann said; "no guardians to think for us, no precedent to follow without question, no lawmaker above, only ordinary men set to deal with heart-breaking perplexity. All weakness comes to the surface. We are homeless in a jungle of machines and untamed powers that haunt and lure our imagination. Of course, our culture is confused, our thinking spasmodic and our emotion out of kilter. No mariner ever enters upon a more uncharted sea than does the average human being, born in the twentieth century. Our ancestors thought they knew their way from birth through all eternity; we are puzzled about day after tomorrow. . . . it is with emancipation that the real tasks begin and liberty is a searching challenge, for it takes away guardianship of the master and the comfort of the priest. The iconoclasts did not free us, they threw us into the water, and now we have to swim."

It was impossible to lay aside the absorbing story of the growth of man's creative mind, and I raced through it avidly. Dawn had begun to break over the mountain peaks when I came to the last paragraph. This time it was James Harvey Robinson speaking to me:

"We must look forward to ever new predicaments and adventures. Nothing is going to be settled in the sense in which things were once supposed to be settled, for the simple reason that knowledge will probably increase and will inevitably alter

[2] Mitchell Kennerly, New York, 1914.

the world with which we have to make terms. . . . we must now substitute purpose for tradition."

The book marked a critical point in my life and opened my eyes to reality. Ever since my husband's death, the secret hope persisted that soon I would remarry and resume my once happy role of wife and mother. Instead, I had been thrust into a world of women and caught in a social upheaval from which there seemed no possibility of escape. Romantic daydreaming was folly. The responsibilities of an unwanted career had to be faced with whatever intelligence I could muster. It was necessary to re-educate myself, to try and understand this wild generation of students, without letting them horrify or intimidate me.

I began to haunt the libraries for books on modern psychology. The works of William James, Freud, Jung, Adler, and Havelock Ellis crowded my shelves. The philosophy of John Dewey and William H. Kilpatrick captured my imagination. I wrestled with old words weighted with new meanings. Identification, sublimation, inferiority complex, extroversion and introversion, infantilism, and many others cluttered my vocabulary. Fearful terms, such as homosexuality and eroticism, cast their evil shadow over abnormal emotional attachments.

One day, as I was browsing, I came upon a thick book called *The Unadjusted Girl*,[3] by W. I. Thomas, a professor of sociology at the University of Chicago. It dealt with the conflicts of adolescence and gave many illustrative cases taken from the files of social workers. The problems of these girls, it seemed to me, differed only in degree from the difficulties of their sisters in the YWCA and in college. It was like discovering a bonanza. The author had reduced the "mechanisms of behavior" to four neat formulas: desires for new experience, security, response, and recognition. Henceforth, I would only have to figure out which

[3] Little, Brown & Co., Boston, 1923.

desire seemed to be motivating the disturbed youngster and then, by some magic as yet beyond my ken, guide her along more settled paths.

Alas, the solution was not so simple! Some recalcitrants had a way of venting all four desires at once, while others added a few that Thomas had failed to mention. At best, my frantic quest for learning had resulted in the acquisition of many provocative books, and just enough psychological information to make me a suspect among preachers, parents, and skeptical instructors. The alumni, ever sensitive to changes, protested that the Dean of Women was making "cases" out of students who happened to get "a little bit out of line," and the president urged me to use caution. "We live in the most conservative belt in the country," he said, "where new methods and ideas are often anathema, no matter how harmless they appear. Let the specialists on the faculty bear the brunt of progress." He was a diplomatic man for whom I had great respect, but he was not a resident of Bemis Hall, and troublesome situations were resolved before they came to his attention. He never knew of my numerous narrow escapes!

Take the time, for instance, when some of the Independent girls petitioned for another literary club. Fraternities had been established on the campus for many years, but sororities were considered too undemocratic for the women. Besides it was believed—the real reason perhaps—that they would wreck the dormitory system which had been a feature of the college since the beginning. In order to satisfy the yearning of the women students to belong to socially exclusive groups, Miss Loomis had suggested a "literary society," and then a second took root, and finally a third. This still left a large number outside the pale, and the time was ripe for a new organization. A committee of girls, petition in hand, came to see me about presenting it to the faculty. The plans were well considered and I was impressed.

Even the name had been chosen: the Lesbian Literary Society of Colorado College. I agreed that it had a pleasant musical tone and was true to tradition in honoring the women of ancient Greece.

But scarcely had the last girl left my living room when something alerted me. It had been a long time since I had slipped through Greek history, in the Cripple Creek High School. Who, exactly, were the Lesbians? Where had I read the name recently—in Ellis, or possibly Freud? I hurried to look it up in the dictionary. The bold definition danced before my eyes and filled me with horror and chagrin:

> *Lesbian—belonging or relating to Lesbos, an island in the Aegean Sea; birthplace of Alcaeus, Arion, Sappho and others of the so-called amatory school; Lesbianism—sensual desire of women for their own sex; Cf. homosexuality. . . .*

The innocent members were stunned when I hastily sent for them and they heard the news. One of the house-mothers had suggested the name—it had sounded so poetical—nobody ever dreamed that such dreadful women existed. I thought they looked at me accusingly, as if I had perpetrated a hoax on them, and I had to confess my own naïveté about the aberrant practices of the ancient Lesbians.

This episode, followed by concentrated readings of Havelock Ellis' *Studies in Sex,* sharpened my awareness of the intense emotional relationships that occasionally developed between certain girls. Often they seemed to be merely transitory, like the crushes that were common in my own undergraduate years. But now and then the infatuation became so serious as to affect the health of one or both of the students involved. The situation was touched on, rather superficially, by the deans in small groups at the state and national meetings, but we were treading on dangerous ground with no one prepared to lead the way. It was simpler to stick to the old paths and ignore the problem. Most of us had come from a generation where sex, no matter how one felt about it in private, was taboo as a subject for public discussion. But the young people of the twenties had no such reservations and sooner or later their elders would have to face the reckoning.

It was after my return from one of these meetings that I decided to seek help outside my profession. I recalled hearing an address at a conference of social workers by Dr. Franklin G. Ebaugh, a noted mental hygienist and director of the Colorado Psychopathic Hospital in Denver. The subject was "Young Girls in Conflict." It made a deep impression on me. As I listened, I wished that the college could arrange to engage him as a consultant. But of course even the suggestion of such a plan would have been ridiculous. Psychiatrists, as everybody knew, treated only the insane and delinquent; nobody would have regarded them as suitable advisers to college deans.

It occurred to me, however, that perhaps he would be willing to let me consult him privately, in case of emergency. My visits would have to be kept secret, and although I had no extra money to spare, I would offer to pay his fee. His office was in a small room in a far wing of the hospital. Photographs of his attractive family hung on the wall. It was a strange sensation to find myself in a hospital for the mentally sick and for a moment I was tempted to flee. The doctor greeted me pleasantly and invited me to sit in a chair by his desk. He was of slight build with kindly blue eyes and a tendency to lisp. Later, when I had come to know him better, he told me that it was his speech defect that had led him into psychiatry as a profession.

He seemed interested to know that a Dean of Women had found the principles of mental hygiene helpful in dealing with student behavior difficulties. I wasted no time in coming to the purpose of my visit. I was in a position of great responsibility and needed enlightenment. The problems threatened to over-whelm me. I wondered if a plan could be worked out whereby I might consult him occasionally when I ran into serious trou-ble——

"Such as——?"

"Well—I don't know how to explain it, but the question of sex, for instance, and the abnormal attachments of girls for each other. I am convinced that many of them are morbid and un-healthy and I am baffled about knowing what to do—I even shrink from what I might hear if a girl should want to confide in me——"

An amused smile crossed his face. "Such practices as you sus-pect are as old as the human race," he said at last, "and in no way peculiar to college girls. They are likely to be found where-ever men or women live in isolated groups. Our knowledge as to the cause is vague. We don't know precisely why some in-dividuals are more attracted sexually to members of their own sex; nor have we found any pat treatment. Sometimes it is a phase of adolescence that soon passes, leaving no permanent damage to the personality."

It struck me that he was too casual about it all. I wanted more specific advice. "I wonder if you would be willing to talk with a student—whom I have in mind—who is failing in her college work and plans to drop out at mid-term because—well—it's very serious."

"That would be impossible for a number of reasons," he said quickly. "I am not in private practice, for one thing, and for an-other you can handle the matter better than I—you are in a key position to be of great help to her. To begin with, you are part of the natural environment of the campus. If you are able to win a young person's confidence there is no limit as to the help you can give her. But first, you must take yourself in hand. It is of the greatest importance for you to lose all squeamishness about sex. Learn to listen—listen to any and everything the troubled student wants to say—listen without feelings of shock, prejudice, or a hint of shame. Try to see behind the words that cause you to shrink; and seek understanding. Above all, avoid increasing the girl's burden of guilt from which, it is certain, she already suffers——"

The telephone was ringing insistently and I got up to leave. He put his hand over the mouthpiece and motioned for me to sit down again. When he had finished the call he turned toward me with a smile and a twinkle in his eyes. "Don't be discouraged by my little sermon," he said. "I am as anxious as you are to see mental hygiene techniques established in every college in the land. It can only happen when deans like you don't make too many mistakes in the beginning." The telephone had begun to ring again and this time he called to a nurse to take the message. "Have you thought of trying to get some special training as a counselor? It has just occurred to me that even one summer's session spent at the New York School of Social Work would be very rewarding for you. Dr. Marion Kenworthy who is on the faculty there has had remarkable success in preparing social workers to straighten out disturbed children and adolescents—as well as their parents. She could give you a point of view and an approach in counseling that would be invaluable. Meanwhile, feel free to come and talk things over when you find yourself in a jam—just phone in advance."

It marked the start of many fruitful discussions with Dr. Ebaugh which changed the course of my thinking. But studying at the School of Social Work was out of the question for the coming summer. I had promised Barbara that we would spend our vacation together in Estes Park and we had already begun to count the days.

V

Two months passed, camping, driving, hiking, and horseback riding over the trails of Estes Park. It was the kind of rugged country I had known as a child and, later, lived in with Howe. I was familiar with all its summer moods when terrifying, purplish clouds hugged the peaks, and lightning ripped through the pines, and rain and hail beat a furious tattoo on cabins and tents. Then the mischievous sun smiled through and we would be off in "Ophelia Bumps" to search for the mushrooms pushing up in the meadows. Sometimes, on the higher, burnt-over slopes we stumbled upon a patch of wild raspberries, or a garden of columbines and pink honeysuckle hidden in a grove of quaking aspens.

How the blue jays chattered and preened their feathers in the warming sun! How fragrant the moist earth when we stopped to drain the radiator and fill it up again with the icy water of the Big Thompson River! "Tomorrow," Barbara said, "let's rent ponies and go to Emerald Lake, or Columbine Lodge, or maybe all the way to the boulder field, above timber line." Tomorrow and tomorrow! Always something to look forward to and talk about. "I like you the way you are in the mountains," she said once, "here you really seem like my mother. Why do we ever have to go back to Bemis Hall?"

It had been two years since Barbara came to live with me in

the college dormitory. Almost from the beginning I realized that it was not the best place for her. She was neither a child nor a grownup, and tried to be both. She saw me preoccupied with other people's daughters. I was seldom there when she came home from school. The round of committee and faculty meetings started at four o'clock and usually lasted until the dinner hour. Or else it was my "day at home," a Loomis custom which I continued, or I might be "pouring" or "receiving" at some reception. More often, I would be talking privately with some troubled student, in my office or living room, while Barbara was at loose ends, frequently hanging around the kitchen and pestering the cooks for snacks. We were separated even at meals. According to tradition, the Dean of Women presided over the senior table, sitting in an imposing chair on a raised platform called the dais. There were no vacant places except when a girl was ill or away for the weekend. Usually Barbara ate with a group of freshmen in the main part of the dining room.

This undesirable situation worried me continuously, and I appealed to the president about the possibility of moving out of the dormitory into a house in town. He was sympathetic but his tone was funereal. Such a radical step would change the character of the college, he said, so far as the Hall girls were concerned. The "resident Dean of Women" had been a feature of Colorado College ever since Miss Loomis first arrived to take charge. The alumni, too, would oppose the plan, and parents might send their daughters elsewhere, thus further cutting down the enrollment. He felt sure that the Board of Trustees would never give its approval. "I am certain," he went on, apparently sensing my disappointment, "that in time the problem can be resolved. For the present, I would suggest that you set up a schedule where two or three hours a day could be devoted to Barbara's needs." I tried this arrangement but with indifferent success; the demands of the position, and unexpected emergencies, took precedence over personal concerns.

The only alternative, it seemed, was to send Barbara to a near-by private school for a year or two while I improved my chances, through study and further experience, for an administrative position in a university where the Dean of Women was not required to "live in." With the exception of the disciplinary duties, I had come to enjoy my work with the undergraduates and, with Dr. Ebaugh's occasional covert help, grew in the understanding of many of their serious conflicts. But I felt troubled about all the empty dormitory rooms. If the advantages of the college were as special as I believed they were, why didn't students scramble to gain admission? A faculty committee decided that the public should be better informed, and, in addition to my other duties, I was selected to go out among the high schools of the state and tell the wonderful story.

No immediate influx of boys and girls responded to my clarion call, but the rewards for me were rich and exciting. I discovered that I had a bent for public speaking; and the seeds of new ideas began to sprout, and my voice evidently had at least the tinkle of authority. My enthusiasm for the generation of stormy young rebels was unbounded and I endowed them with gifts their parents never suspected. Whatever the effect may have been upon my listeners, it was tonic for me, and I always returned to the college inspired and refreshed by my own speeches. This was a fortunate antidote against the problems my assistant, Miss Majorie Crouch, had piled up during my absence. A few were as amusing as they were bothersome.

For instance, there was that prank one early April. I had arrived home, after a long tiring journey, at five o'clock in the morning. An Alpine glow tinged the snowy pate of Pike's Peak and frosty air nipped my fingers as I fumbled for change to pay the cab driver. All I could think of was crawling under warm blankets as quickly as possible and stealing a bit more sleep before the rising bell rang. Suddenly a shadowy figure loomed out of the dawn, just in front of the door. For a second my heart stood still. I was afraid I had lost my mind from weariness. A life-size African lion was crouching there, guarding the entrance! Its jaws hung open and I imagined I could hear a low snarl. We faced each other for what seemed like eternity. Then I noticed in the spreading light a monkey hanging from one of the branches of a maple tree, while a stately giraffe nibbled at the twigs. Something familiar about the lion led me to reach out and touch his mane. Sure enough, it was moth-eaten and mangy from standing for years on an imitation boulder in the college museum.

I went over to the maple tree for a closer look at the giraffe and monkey, and then decided to go on a stealthy safari up the road past Ticknor Hall and across Cascade Avenue to the main campus. What a menagerie met my astonished gaze! They were all there, ready for a frolic—the golden eagle perched on the flagpole, the anteater, coyote, and leopard feeding on dead grass, the buffalo, polar bear, and Rocky Mountain goat contemplating the scene through glassy eyes. All at once I saw the huge Brontosaurus, the curator's prize exhibit, stretched in reptilian splendor, almost full length in front of Palmer Hall.

By now a small crowd was gathering. Everybody chuckled and laughed, except the curator who had just put in an appearance. It was evident from his florid face that he saw nothing funny in the situation. He paced among the onlookers, as if trying to flush out the perpetrators of the outrage. "If one bone in that dinosaur's spine is cracked," he fumed, "those vandals will be punished if it's the last act of my life!" But the pranksters were not caught in spite of faculty investigations. Indeed, they would probably never be known until years hence when some distinguished alumnus returned to receive an honorary degree

and regaled the audience with the hilarious tale about the time
he and his fraternity brothers pastured the beasts and birds from
the college museum all around the peaceful, pre-dawn campus.

Back in Bemis Hall the atmosphere was serene; it seemed to
me that the girls looked unusually fresh and innocent. Thank
heaven, I said to myself, they weren't involved in the crazy an-
tic! Or were they? A certain blandness in their smiles gave me
pause. I was aware that young people were fiercely loyal to each
other in a crisis, knowing, perhaps, that adults were apt to line
up against them. But I was not going to pry into the affair.
Jessie had come to get me—another, more urgent problem demanded my attention.

For two or three weeks before I left on my trip, some of the
girls had complained of losing costume jewelry and small sums
of money from their rooms while they were at class. I gave little
credence to the reports at first and blamed the losses on careless-
ness. Probably there weren't any intentional thefts; the possessions had simply been misplaced. Also the habit of lending and
borrowing clothes and other belongings had become a common
practice in the dormitories. I explained how easy it was to go
from borrowing a party dress or a hat to taking a matching handbag. If by chance the purse contained a little change, or a bill
or two, and the friend happened to be short of funds, she might
use the money with the intention of repaying it when she received her allowance. And occasionally such things slipped her
memory.

But I was conscious of not sounding very convincing either
to the girls or to myself. Actually I shrank from coming to grips
with the ugly business. The very thought of laying a trap to
catch one of the dormitory students repelled me. It might be
that lovable senior who often sat next to me at dinner; or possibly
the forlorn-looking sophomore who waited on table and for whom
I had recently secured a loan; or it could turn out to be Penny—

or Meg—or Becky—or any of the others who danced with such gay abandon after dinner in the Commons. The atmosphere of the house became tremulous with suspicion. Roommates distrusted each other. Where did Margie get the cash for her new spring outfit? How could Ella-Jane afford to go to the movies so often? Rumors were rife and simple words grew heavy with innuendoes. I had used every excuse to avoid a showdown, until it struck me that I was losing something more important than money—the confidence of the girls who had appealed to me for help.

Plainly I had to do something about it before leaving. I decided to talk, in utmost secrecy, with Cynthia and Anne, two of the students who had suffered most from the thefts, and proposed a detailed plan. Lately the purloiner had begun to raid rooms during the breakfast hour, which made it a little easier to snare her. Cynthia volunteered to be the victim. Several dollar bills would be marked and placed in full view in a handbag lying open on the bed, while she and Anne hid in the closet, with the door slightly ajar. They were to do this for a week, or until the thief showed up again. In that case, they were to bring her to me at once or call my assistant in case I hadn't returned to town.

Unluckily for me, the two sleuths, looking pale and distraught, caught their prey the very morning of the raid on the college museum and stood guard over her in my living room until Jessie came after me. The girl couldn't have been more frightened than I was, as we sat facing each other on the couch, alone with a dreadful situation. Her name was Sophie and she lived on a dry farm several miles east of town. I recalled having sent for her a few times in connection with her low grades in mathematics. Beyond that, I knew little about her except that she was plain, inept in manner, and had an unforgettable gleam of defiance in her steady blue eyes.

Just now she seemed surprisingly self-possessed and spoke freely of her plight. Her brother drove her to town every day for an eight o'clock class in mathematics, she said, but often she had cut it because she hated math and hadn't prepared the lessons. This left her with time to kill and she decided to explore the dormitories. "At first I only meant to walk through them," she went on, "to see how other girls lived. Then I peeked into some of the rooms. So many things were lying around—nice things like beads and rings. And there was money, too, loose change and bills, scattered on dressers—after a while the money was all I took. I didn't think those kids would ever miss it. I put it in a savings bank at home, to buy myself a new coat. The folks never knew——" Her voice broke suddenly, her chin quivered, and she collapsed against me, sobbing, "Please don't tell my mother—oh please—expel me if you want to, or send me to jail, but don't tell my folks!"

I managed to calm her at last and tried to convince her that I had no other choice: I would have to call her mother and Sophie could tell the story in her own words—better that way than have it come from the lips of strangers. It was a heartbreaking scene, but the incredulous mother played her part with great courage and understanding. She asked me to assure the students that her daughter would return every cent of the money and any other things she had taken. Then she looked at me helplessly and begged that Sophie be spared disgrace. "Let her finish the few weeks left of the semester," she pleaded, "and you'll not have to worry about her any more. Sophie is a fine girl who made a bad mistake—she's learned a terrible lesson."

Sophie did stay on for the rest of the college term and came by every week or so to see me. She planned to go to Berkeley in the fall and live with an aunt while she studied at the university. She had determined to major in psychology and prepare herself for social work. It was a happy ending to a tragic experience for Sophie, but for me it was only the beginning of such ordeals. The problem of petty stealing was perennial, no matter how large or small the college, nor where it happened to be located. And the solution was not always so gratifying.

My first few years as Dean of Women had been largely ventures in disillusionment. I soon got rid of the idea that success depended on my ability to please everybody—trustees, faculty, alumni, parents, and students, to say nothing of the Ministerial Alliance. Seldom did these various groups expect the same things of a college administrator. She was supposed to be a "glorified housekeeper," a scholar, a preserver of sainted traditions, and a good sport. I discovered that wide popularity was not only impossible but dangerous as a goal and that sound criticism could be a bracer. It occurred to me, too, that it was human nature to seek an object of atonement, to focus anger and bitterness on some single individual in authority, no matter how innocent he might have been. This thought often gave me a wholesome feeling of detachment in a critical hour.

I began to suspect that to other people we were all images of one kind or another. The Dean of Women was the symbol of power among the students, and of all the roles I had to play, this was the most difficult. In the limited area of the college campus, every word I uttered was loaded with undue importance. Hidden clues and meanings seemed to lie in my simplest remarks. Sometimes the students, noted for their peculiar sense of humor, would turn them into jokes for the end men at the junior minstrel show. It took constant vigilance to restrain my natural spontaneity. Once I happened to mention this worry to a minister. I never forgot his advice. "Be sure your heart is right," he said, "and you'll never be troubled about the words of your mouth."

But unhappily I could not always trust my heart, and the inability to communicate freely, even with my young daughter, deepened my sense of isolation and loneliness. Memories of Miss Loomis came back to haunt me. I began to understand, at last, why she had kept aloof and impersonal. We never seemed to regard her as a human being, much like ourselves, only more grownup and independent. How little we appreciated her many deeds of kindness, always unknown until some one of us had become the beneficiary! I remembered one evening in my senior year, after both my mother and father had died, and I was very much in need of new clothes. She had slipped an envelope under my door while I was at dinner, and inside were two five-dollar bills. "To go toward the coat—from an anonymous friend." I recognized her gray notepaper and the neat, vertical handwriting.

All through the years the recollection of what she did for me has remained vivid. But I doubted if, at the time, I had expressed adequate thanks. Now, seeing the opportunities through her eyes, I knew that she had been "anonymous friend" to countless other students, and that their gratefulness was likely to have been as meager as their praise and she never showed any sign of expecting it. But I was not so secure in my position, nor in myself, as Miss Loomis. I wanted the reassurance of appreciation and found it hard to understand when it so seldom came. But I recalled something that Dr. Ebaugh had told me one day in connection with Penny, who had accepted so much, as if it were her due. "Appreciation," he said, with the slight lisp that had endeared him to me, "usually comes with maturity. Some people never attain it; they remain all their lives at the level of adolescence."

I had worn down many a tire on "Ophelia Bumps," driving back and forth on the rough, gravelly road to Denver for sessions with him. His patience was endless and I owed him a great deal for the enlightenment he never failed to give me. But he was rapidly becoming a leader in the National Association of Mental Hygiene and attended many conventions and conferences, in addition to his hospital responsibilities. He was no longer so easily available. I, too, was out in the field, making speeches and attending teachers' conventions, and then rushing back to the many college problems that awaited me. And always, in the spring, I journeyed to the big annual conference of the National Association of Deans of Women, which met in cities like Dallas, Chicago, Washington, and Boston.

It was a busy life, but there was plenty of time for thinking as I traveled on slow trains and laid over in tank towns. More and more, it struck me that I was spinning in circles, getting nowhere, and making no headway toward realizing the longed-for home. Except for a wide acquaintance, and a few close friends among college deans and presidents, my travels had netted little in the way of valuable experience. Soon I would be caught in a hopeless rut, I thought dismally, going around and around, trying to fill up the empty dormitory rooms. What a dreary prospect!

Further study couldn't be put off any longer. I would have to spend the coming summer at the New York School of Social Work. Barbara was not as disappointed as I had feared when I told her that I was going to send her to the Perry-Mansfield Camp at Steamboat Springs, high in the Rockies. Already she had decided that someday she was going to be a great actress, and this camp made a specialty of teaching dramatics, along with swimming and horseback riding. "We'll go again soon to Estes Park," I said, feeling rather sorry for myself. The vague dread of what I had come to think of as the boarding school-summer camp routine began to weigh on me, and I almost broke down when I saw her waving happily from the train window, bound for two months among the thespians at the Perry-Mansfield Camp.

VI

The six weeks of study in New York were absorbing and difficult. I had to learn to work as I had never worked before and, even then, fell short of the long assignments in writing and reading. Dr. Kenworthy illustrated her lectures with cases taken from her records, and I could have sworn that she had filched them from my confidential files. But the new wave of psychiatric terms engulfed me, and courage dwindled in the face of my vast ignorance. I wondered how I could have been so artless as to think that a brief period in the School of Social Work would make up for all the knowledge I lacked. It became clearer than ever that if the home of which I dreamed were to become a reality, I had better get out of college work as quickly as possible.

I decided to stay an extra week in New York and make the rounds of a few advertising firms. But in spite of glowing letters of introduction I never got beyond the receptionist. Then I remembered a note a friend had given me to the widow of a famous sociologist and writer. In the few years since her husband's death, she had achieved a notable career selling bonds, and my friend felt sure that she could give me some valuable counsel and might even know of an opportunity in publicity for a woman of my background.

Her office was up two steep flights of stairs in an old building on lower Fifth Avenue. I grew more and more nervous as I hurried up the steps, and by the time her desk was reached I was gasping for breath. She was a small well-tailored woman with dark hair and piercing black eyes. I had an instant suspicion that I was in the wrong place and wondered how to make a graceful exit. She listened, coldly, as I elaborated on my publicity accomplishments with the Young Women's Christian Association. I also spoke of the public relations and speaking I had done for Colorado College. It was the residence requirement, I went on to explain, that made me discontented in my position as Dean of Women, and I wished to make a home for my daughter. It had occurred to me that I might learn the business of selling bonds. Would she be so kind as to give me suggestions?

A sardonic smile crossed her lips, and she tapped the desk with her pencil, as if annoyed. "Evidently you don't know the difficulties of trying to get a job in New York. You would be lost here, in no time. You have to know the ropes—selling bonds is highly competitive. Besides," she said, pointing the pencil at me for emphasis, *"that's* very much against you——"

"I don't understand," I said, quaking like a leaf and fearing that my dress had come unbuttoned. "What do you mean?"

"This panting for breath—is something wrong with your heart?"

"Certainly not—it's just that I hurried up the stairs too fast."

"Bond sellers have to climb lots of stairs," she said, "and short-windedness would be a distinct handicap. My advice is that you stay in the pleasant, peaceful work you are doing as a Dean of Women—there are dozens of fine boarding schools where you could send your daughter." She pushed back her chair as if to end the interview. "How I envy you living in such a delightful place as Colorado Springs. I spent a few weeks there once——"

I never knew how I made it back down those wicked steps for I was still in a daze when I reached the sidewalk. It was my first and last attempt to storm the barbed walls of New York City's business world. But the venture reconciled me, at least temporarily, to the topsy-turvy delights of life in Bemis Hall, where politeness was the password and I was a person of no mean importance.

But in spite of the news that the enrollment had increased and most of the dormitory rooms had been assigned, a feeling of depression clung to me. Even the president's assurance that my high school visits helped do the trick failed to lift my spirits. I shrank from the joyous squeals of students greeting each other after the long vacation and winced at the nerve-wracking click, click, click of spike heels on the floor above my living room. The literary societies were getting ready for the rush season, and, with more prospects to choose from, excitement reached a sharp pitch. I looked forward with dread to the hectic days.

Prosperity surged through the nation and a different kind of undergraduate roamed the campus. Parents who had formerly regarded higher education as a luxury, especially for their daughters, now spoke of it as a necessity. A degree, they were told, would prepare a young woman to earn a living, if need be, in some calling such as teaching or library work, until she married. Still more current was the belief that going to college would give a girl social prestige, particularly if she happened to join a favored sorority or a literary society. And woe to the hapless freshman who failed to make any of them!

Often the rejected ones, looking crushed and tearful, landed in my living room. I tried to comfort and reason with them but never felt convincing. I myself had once been an unthinking party to the cruel system. It would have made me as wretched as the students who wept on my shoulder now to have been left out of a society when I was a freshman. "I've been judged and found wanting," a forlorn girl would say, "please tell me what is wrong with me—if I only knew—maybe I could change and be like the others."

Frequently it was the blow to family pride that caused the most worry. "My mother will be heartbroken when she hears it," another would sob, "she counted on my making a society and now I've let her down—how can she ever face her friends!" Through the perspective of years, I tried to show how superficial the judgments were, how little it really mattered whether one belonged to this or that social group; how much more important it was to develop one's own individuality and not flock with the crowd. But one glance at a pair of stricken eyes made me realize how meaningless my words had been.

But youth is resilient and wounded spirits are quick to heal. Sometimes the rebuff seemed to act as a spur to a girl's ultimate membership in Phi Beta Kappa, the most distinguished and exclusive society in college. Such was Maria, the daughter of a Hungarian miner up in Leadville. Except for winning a freshman scholarship, it would have been impossible for her to continue her education. Her hair was golden yellow, and her eyes were as blue as the Colorado sky on a summer morning. But she lacked the savoir-faire and self-assurance that separated the "literary society material" from the ordinary run of young human beings. The fact that she had to wait on table to earn part of her expenses seemed to deepen her natural shyness and evident feeling of inferiority.

At first, her strong arms managed the heavy trays as if they were a challenge. The dietitian reported that she was quick, reliable, and co-operative. I often noticed her with admiration from my throne on the dais. But her manner changed the day the society bids came out, and no little white envelope was slipped under Maria's door. Her face grew sullen and she shoved the plates onto the table as if she wanted to smash them. I made a point of trying to chat with her whenever we met in the halls, but she hurried on, unsmiling, as though tears lay near the surface.

One Sunday afternoon in late September I invited her to go driving with me in my Ford. We chugged up the steep grade of Ute Pass through Woodland Park and, before I realized it, we had come to the small outpost of Divide, only twelve or fifteen miles from Cripple Creek. The western foothills of Pike's Peak shimmered with the autumn gold of quaking aspens. In the distant southwest, we could see Mount Pisgah and Bull Cliff rising like sentries guarding the old mining camp that sprawled in the basin below. I knew the country well; the slopes and gulches and high meadows had been my playgrounds. I told Maria about having lived there as a child, during the gold rush, and how my father, after many years of hardship and prospecting with a divining rod, had finally made a strike that enabled me to go to college.

"I was a sophomore when my mother died," I went on, observing her interest, "and then I lost my father just before the start of my senior year."

"In a mine accident?"

"No; consumption—he had been sick with it a long time, and his money was all gone. I was about to give up the idea of ever finishing college. Then a miracle happened. My father's friends, mostly miners, contributed enough to make graduation possible."

"Miners did that for you?"

"For my father," I corrected. "They were strangers to me, except for Griff Lewis, the druggist, who sent the money orders every month. The donations were collected in a fishbowl marked "For John's Girl," which was placed on top of his drugstore showcase."

"Well, what do you know!" she said, and lapsed into silence.

"The lesson it taught me was worth more than my degree," I said, turning the car and heading back down the Pass. "I learned to value people for what they were like on the inside, not by the roughness of their hands. Until then, I had always been a bit ashamed of my prospector father. I didn't understand such things as a man's integrity and honor."

"Thank you for telling me that story," she said at last. "I can't tell you what it has meant to me. In Leadville, Hungarians are called 'Hunkies' and I was always trying to live it down. I even blamed my father for my not getting a bid, but now I guess it doesn't really matter. Perhaps there are other goals ahead."

Such moments, and there were many of them, lightened my burden of responsibility. The blue chiffon party dress found, somehow, for the pretty daughter of an impecunious minister; the emergency loan wangled from the tight-fisted trustee for a senior whose father had been killed in one of his mines; the vigil kept with the family of a dying girl. These and many other opportunities, common among Deans of Women everywhere, so I discovered, lifted my sights from routine defeats and discouragements and enriched my days.

But one gnawing hunger, a kind of insatiable longing for companionship, persisted. All the girls crowding my life never could make up for the yearning for my daughter. It often turned my gaiety into an aching sense of frustration. The men with whom I danced at the college parties were students almost young enough to be my sons. Or else they were faculty members whose agility lay in their brains rather than their feet. And the wives were usually wrapped up in family concerns and the small economies of running a household on a meager income. There were few of my own age with whom to relax and take off my proper disguise for a little while.

As compensation, I acquired the habit of reading late, after the dormitory had grown quiet. One night a momentous thing happened although I did not realize it at the time. I was leafing through a new copy of the *Atlantic Monthly* and came upon a story called "A Conversation With Cornelia"[1] by Stuart P. Sherman, the chairman of the English Department at the University of Illinois. I began it mostly out of curiosity, possibly because I once had a dear friend named Cornelia. But before long I was stirred with a mixture of envy and indignation. The story savored more of truth than fiction. The interlocutor happened to be a professor at the local university and a long-time, bachelor friend of Cornelia and her husband, Oliver. Their two model children, a boy and girl of teen age, called him uncle. Often he dined with Cornelia when Oliver was called out of town. The professor's flowery description led me to suspect that he was more than halfway in love with her:

> *She was a young woman of forty-five, with a coronet face, finely cut and proudly borne; it gives one distinction merely to be in her presence. Married to a chevalier of the diplomatic corps—an excellent alliance—she has walked ever since between purple rivers. Her ways have gone smoothly and well, in delectable regions far above the rank-scented multitude. When one talks with her, her hands lie still in her lap, nor does any other emphasis of her body intrude its comment upon the serene and assured movements of her intelligence. So remote, she seems, from the ignominious and infamous aspects of existence that one wonders how she becomes aware of them. Yet such unpleasant things, verminous or reptilian, as creep within range of her vision she inspects sharply and with intrepidity, for she knows precisely how to deal with them——*

It was not the poetic allusions to Cornelia's virtues that annoyed me. It was his uncritical acceptance of her opinions. She thoroughly disapproved of the modern woman who willingly

[1] *Atlantic Monthly*, January 1924.

sacrificed marriage for what she called a career. Such misguided females, she averred, were setting a bad example for the youth of today who seemed to be flaunting time-worn social traditions and standards of morality. They clamored for men's professions and equal rights in sex, said Cornelia, whose own ways had gone "smoothly and well in delectable regions far above the level of the rank-scented multitude." They were mistaking license for freedom and trying to compete in a world where love, too, had become an object of trade——

My resentment mounted; it was more than I could endure. Here was a person, I thought, who had never suffered the pain of loneliness. Her "coronet face" had not been lined with worry about money, or home and children. She had in Oliver the attributes that mattered in a husband—devotion, wit, and a distinguished post. He was the kind who would take her in his arms when she happened to feel out of sorts and give her restoring comfort and assurance.

I was suddenly moved to enlighten Stuart Sherman about the modern woman as I had come to know her. A wicked compulsion to shock him and his Cornelia right out of their ivory towers took possession of me. I tossed the magazine aside and reached for my writing pad. "Tonight," I began, "I am conversing with you as an ordinary woman, a bit more daring than usual, but in all honesty. Your portrait of Cornelia disturbs me. Do you actually believe that her views are authentic? Her narrow path has never crossed mine. She simply does not exist for me. Her hands are too white as they 'lie still in her lap,' her bearing is aloof. She is clean, like a clean window that one should not touch. I suspect that in a moment of frankness, Oliver might be so indiscreet as to agree with me, that she is lacking in warmth and charm. But, of course, by now he had become used to her ways.

"This model that you have created," I continued, unconsciously, "stands for a kind of life that has become old fashioned and is foreign to me. She is an orthodox creed in which I no longer believe, a platform which I cannot support, a moral code to which I do not always adhere. Tell Cornelia, for me, that few women have gone into careers from choice. Seldom is one found who would not give up her job, or position, no matter how successful she may be, or how glamorous her achievement, if a man, say, of Oliver's stamp, should ask her to be his wife. Often she would gladly settle for less. And what if the chance to marry never came, must she forever sublimate her desire for completion? Or should she go adventuring in a secret garden where even the flowers may wither and die, that she might find brief fulfillment as a woman?

"It is midnight," I wrote finally. "When I waken in the morning, I shall find myself back in the kitchen of life, watering the red geraniums that are trying to bloom in my casement window. Perhaps I am the reincarnation of Willa Cather's 'Lost Lady' and just beyond the Mesa, some Lothario may be coming to put my virtue to the test. I wonder—was that an 'arrowy smile' that just softened Cornelia's dark eyes?" It was signed "Patricia Thorne."

I felt relieved and a bit frightened as I turned off the light. The uninhibited Cripple Creek girl had escaped from the prison of Bemis Hall, and for a fleeting hour had come alive once again. It had been risky, I realized, to involve the Dean of Women in such an escapade. For a moment, I was tempted to destroy the letter; already it had served a useful purpose. Why interrupt a busy professor's life? But it was not likely that he would read my outpouring words, much less feel obligated to reply. So I decided to seal the envelope and took it myself to the post office the next morning. Then I asked my student-secretary to refer to me any mail that might come addressed to Patricia Thorne.

VII

I never actually doubted that Stuart Sherman would someday acknowledge my rash criticisms of his Cornelia, but I was not prepared for a reply by return mail. Already the memory of my escape into brief adventure had begun to fade, as if it might have been only a dream. And now, here I was face to face with the truth of my folly. My hands trembled as I tore open the envelope and saw "My Dear Patricia Thorne" written in the cramped, meticulous style of a scholarly university professor. A feeling of dismay seized me at the thought of my deception. The name was a mockery, made up out of whole cloth in a moment of recklessness—a "thorne" in the side of decorum. What if he had seen through the ruse! Half curious, half dreading, I read on:

Someday I shall write a story about you and your romance. It will be fiction because I don't believe there is anyone just like Patricia Thorne. You came in this morning like a character in a story, bringing the scenery with you, and the suspense, and the mystery. I can see you in your house on the mesa at the foot of the mountains, waiting—and while you wait, writing that quite charming meditation on Cornelia.

You were most hospitable to take me into the confidence of Patricia Thorne's midnight reflections in the capacity of a mere human being. And I am going to reciprocate by a confidence which you will not, I hope, divulge widely. In the small town world which most of us inhabit it contributes to whatever interest Cornelia arouses to have it conjectured that the lady is a picture of my wife or my grandmother.

But to you I confide that Cornelia is in reality a picture of a "lobe" of my brain, dressed up something like a lady and held off at arm's length so that I can look at her from another critical lobe, which finds her in some respects quite amusing and in most respects out of touch with the sense of life represented in her own children. Whatever you say in adverse criticism of her, there is a critical sense to receive with welcome and docility, a critical sense which is listening with sympathy and the liveliest curiosity to whatever Cornelia's children or other adventurers are willing to reveal about their explorations of felicity.

Your letter piques my interest because it contains a certain note of elation from which you intimate a conviction that Cornelia is shut out. Well, I'm deeply curious about that, about all that you intimate of the charm and spiritual growth that may come from roots running into a secret garden. I am curious to know whether those qualities which a thirsty soul seeks when it ventures out of its solitude, can be nourished by roots in a secret garden.

Most women are incomprehensible to me. I can understand what you say of the normal woman's hunger to be loved. But I can't quite understand what seems to be pretty nearly the average woman's willingness to be loved by anybody and everybody.

That is one criticism which my vertical lobe makes on the "life of adventure," for which the younger generation seems going on.

The second criticism is this: You speak of a "divine pas-

sion." Is it not a fact that the divine passion when it is secure, is a most isolated and exclusive passion? Is it not the essence of such passion to feel: "You and I are alone in the universe —sufficient unto each other—as much alone as if we were the sole created beings?"

Well, there are no such isolated souls in the universe—or virtually none. Therefore, their "divine feeling" is due either to 1) romantic illusion or 2) inhuman callousness to the pull of vital human relationships amid which they have undertaken to plant their Paradise—their solitude à deux. In either case, the charm seems always in danger of discovering implications of ugliness and cruelty.

That is about the present state of my enquiry into the possibilities of the rather human relationship which interests you. Whether the danger can be evaded, whether there is good news of success from adventurers with an earned right to speak is what I would like to know. I should be glad to hear more about the red geraniums.

Very sincerely yours,
Stuart P. Sherman.

My immediate reaction to this long, beautifully written letter was one of chagrin. The Dean of Women looked askance at Patricia Thorne, and I was torn between them. I had read enough psychology to know that I had unwittingly revealed too much of my own smoldering problem—unfulfillment as a woman. No romance waited for me beyond the mesa; no flowers bloomed in a secret garden. My purpose had been to provoke the author who seemed to know so little about the facts of a woman's life. I hoped to make Cornelia's fine feathers ruffle in righteous indignation. It had been a way of rebelling against the circumstances that had warped my own existence. Stuart Sherman probably recognized Patricia Thorne as a sham and had written out of amusement, expecting to uncover her pretensions. Why had I been so foolhardy as to write him? Questions of moral philosophy were plainly over my head. I might have known that a college professor would lead me into such a trap, and I resolved not to answer him.

But the temptation was too great for a person of Patricia's temperament. She began to take over again, reasoning that I had brought it on myself, and the only courteous thing to do was to acknowledge his letter with whatever grace and gaiety I could muster. With that out of the way, I could go about my daily lot of watering the red geraniums running riot in my casement window. And at the moment, several were demanding attention. For instance, there was the problem of animals, erroneously called "pets," which seemed to be over-running the halls like ants in spring. Kittens were born in student rooms, puppies barked at night, and the clean smell of varnish in the corridors had given way to a mixture of unpleasant odors. Jessie came to me with tales of woe; the dietitian threatened to quit because of food taken from the dining room. It was astonishing how a few dogs and cats could upset the dormitory system at Colorado College. Unfortunately, I had to play the role of judge, jury, and executioner—with the valuable support of Baylis, the superintendent of buildings and grounds.

But even more bothersome was the epidemic of romances that had swept the campus. Fraternity pins changed bosoms so often it was hard to keep up with the engaged girls. According to custom, when one became "pinned" she was entitled to more lenient considerations on the part of the Dean of Women and student government. Faculty members complained that the "excessive necking" had become a sort of racket that was playing havoc with studies. They urged that I make a rule against the travesty on love, and require that the engagement have the official stamp of approval from the girl's parents. I made an honest

attempt to check the plague but found that the mothers were
not always co-operative. Apparently they did not object to their
daughters' hobby of collecting fraternity pins, but rather looked
upon it as the mark of a girl's popularity. "By the time Helen
is a senior," a parent told me, "she should be an experienced
judge of men; that's one reason why we sent her to a coeducational college."

My sympathies, too, were with the students, but for a different reason. The reflected glow of romance had warmed my
own life. The jasmine in my secret garden was shedding a sweet
fragrance. I began to look forward, more and more, to my literary trysts with Cornelia's creator. The veil of anonymity gave
me release from the tradition-bound garments of the Dean of
Women. I could speak freely, no matter how shocking the
words. The writing itself filled me with a certain exaltation, as
if I were tapping riches from a hidden bonanza. Stuart Sherman seemed to sense this and led me on:

*You have a quality which I prize highly—joy [he wrote].
Is it real? Why are you happy? There is something conta-
gious in joy of this quality. It is a good in itself. What other
means do you find of expressing it? I place the vocation of
joy at the top of all human callings. It doesn't require any
other quality or justification. You write with personality and
distinction. What other ways have you found for expressing
your joy? I am curious about that, and if you want to tease
my curiosity further, you will drop another hint. You see I am
engaged in a quest. I want to find out why the average
American is so miserable; why he lives such a poverty
stricken existence in his personal relations; why he goes about
with uncommunicable hunger in his soul. I believe that I
shall find the answer by consulting joyous persons. If you
are one, tell me about it, please.*

I could not tell him—not yet—that my joy was as deceptive as my pseudonym, and that it was only his imagination that gave it reality. I was another "lobe" of his brain which he had dressed up something like a joyous person. I flinched from destroying the beautiful illusion. Deans of Women, below the rank of professor, were not usually held in high regard by the elite in faculty circles. Few of them held graduate degrees; their attributes were looked upon as disciplinarian in nature, as social rather than intellectual. I suspected that in a large university the distinctions would be even more sharply drawn, and that confessing my lowly status to the chairman of the Department of English would have meant sudden death to Patricia Thorne.

I decided to keep her alive until I had teased his curiosity a bit longer. Possibly then he would be better able to accept the revelation. But already his letters began to express doubts.

I really suspect you to be someone in masquerade [he said], engaged on her own little quest of curiosity, to discover what manner of being writes that stuff for magazines. In your first letter, I took you for one of Browning's ladies, living with a still intensity within a ring of fire. But later, I began to detect a skillful masquerader bent on an amusive quest. Has the "higher criticism" failed in both instances?

But still I lacked sufficient courage to take off my disguise. He knew, of course, that I lived in a college town, and that my address, Bemis Hall, could easily be one of the campus buildings. He might even suspect that I was a teacher. But Dean of Women—no! He was willing to bide his time, evidently, and appease his curiosity with a more roundabout approach.

An escapade, like this exchange of letters [he wrote], will soon die of inanition if it is not fed. I should like to suggest some lavender which you may use to feed and perfume the flowers. I am giving you a commission. My editor, Ellery Sedgwick, telegraphed me this morning that he is "desperately in love with Cornelia" and that I must get her to talk on two or three other topics which he suggested, among them, the kind of man that one should desire one's daughter to marry. This sounds like a Ladies' Home Journal subject; but Cornelia should discuss it with a certain difference.

Do you know anything about daughters? Can you tell me what the latest thing in a man is, for a woman who really has an ideal for her personal life? Can you put this into your dancing words? Or does he exist on land or sea? I am by conviction a remorseless realist, myself. I care less and less for dream men and dream women. But if the shape of one's dream exists in the flesh, if there is reality correspondent to the desire, that is news of the first importance. Let us tell "these young people" what to seek for to the bitter end. Let us not tell them, however, to wait for dreams.

Have I lifted the latch? Is there anyone at home?

SS

P.S. Since you address me as "Professor," it is needless to make allusion to the routine in which this letter is an interlude. But by way of reciprocity, would you not when you write again, put a bit of scenery behind your masquerade by annotating a little what you call "the busy round of my days?"

It was a baffling assignment. I read it over and over with a trace of annoyance. Was Stuart Sherman trying to pinpoint me, hoping that I would give myself away? I made many attempts to answer, but the "dancing words" were inadequate. The Dean of Women was peering over my shoulder and whispering such terms as intelligence, integrity, kindness, patience —these were the traits to seek in the "ideal man." But there were qualities beyond them which Patricia called vitality, humor, and, yes, sex appeal—that magnetic quality so seldom mentioned by ladies of Cornelia's stamp. Then suddenly, in exasperation, I decided to abandon my double life and to make an honest woman out of the Dean. Perhaps, with a fair and easy conscience, I could think more clearly and stop playing games with my superior opponent. Let come what would, he must know the kind of thwarted person it was who tried to win him away from the lady of the "coronet face" who "walked between purple rivers." The thought of never hearing from him again gave me pause. But in a few days the familiar handwriting once again marked an envelope on my desk——

My Dear Patricia [*his reply began*]:

I have decided to adhere to this name in the hope that there is a being somehow connected with the word who will answer this letter.

But to be candid, I was at first terribly shocked to discover, though I had suspected it from the beginning, that you were not a free spirit but of all created spirits, the most strictly straightened, cribb'd, cabin'd and confin'd. I had thought, you see, that you had news of a territory outside the domain of "perfect behavior"—real news. To hear then, that it came from the citadel of perfect behavior was disheartening. At first, it seemed just fiction and dream-stuff, such as drifts up from any speculative pipe and mingles with the smoke in even academic studies. Well, I have recovered from that, and having pondered the point, now conclude that Patricia's case is even more interesting than before, because more typical, more representative of the average estate. And I have concluded, too, that I needn't despair of real news, either, from the Citadel of Perfect Behavior. All the ro-

*mances of the Middle Ages present us with princesses and
wandering knights imprisoned in strong dungeons—till some
trumpet blast announces the coming of a deliverer.*

How grateful I was to know that the Dean of Women had
not lost caste with the Professor! The letters continued still with
the relish of an adventure. And as winter passed into spring
our discussions were reflected in the further "conversations"
with Cornelia which appeared from time to time in the *Atlantic.* We covered the ground from daughters, their education
and careers, to theories of happiness and how they differed from
the real thing. Again and again I was thrust into a corner, trying to defend the beauty and vitality of the inner life, which
Stuart Sherman maintained never existed until it had become
externalized in some artistic form or useful activity.

It struck me, as I read the published essays, that a change
had come over Cornelia. She was more tolerant of "cooks and
dressmakers," and less opinionated. Her teen-age children, so
carefully trained, had even become involved with Prohibition
and a motor accident, and Cornelia faced a few of the facts
of youth that she had been overlooking. For a while, it seemed
that a kind of estrangement had developed between her and
Oliver, her husband, and privately I warned Stuart Sherman
not to go calling on her so frequently—that people would talk.
Apparently he himself had begun to have doubts about her per-
fections. "I wonder," he confessed in one of his letters,
"whether she, too, doesn't wear a mask; whether she, too, isn't
shamming; whether if one really knew her to the core, there
would not be found there—at the core—the same irrational, hot,
passional hungers and discontents and satisfactions as those of
her house maid." Then he added, "I do not wish to allege her
mistress of a civilization and culture to which she hasn't really
attained."

Poor Cornelia! I was stricken with a sense of remorse. What had I done to her by disillusioning her old family friend? And how could I be sure that my own opinions were not colored by a mining-camp background, about which I had kept Stuart Sherman in the dark? I was aware, also, of certain changes in my own thinking. Secret gardens had lost their charm for me, and romance was not confined to affairs of the heart. The gifted teacher and writer had reached across the plains from his university study to mellow my understanding and lighten the burden of my isolation. "A free soul," he said, "may just chance to find that her happiness lies most truly in conforming with certain external standards—the thing to remember is that all of the precious values of life are found in expression—and may be treated as art."

Near Easter, a brief note came saying that he was going to New York to look at a position "which might conceivably promise a little more margin for growth of what is inside." Shortly afterward he accepted the editorship of *Books*, the book section of the New York *Herald Tribune*. The distance between us had widened, but he had not forgotten Patricia Thorne. One morning I found a letter on my Bemis Hall desk from the editor of the *Atlantic Monthly*. It read:

Dear Mrs. Lee:

    Will you pardon the indiscretion of an editor who learned his conventions many years ago?

    My friend, Professor Sherman, the discriminating admirer of Cornelia, told me in friendly conversation the other night of some correspondence which he had with you. What he said, caught and held my attention, and I have asked him whether I might make bold to write and inquire whether—if necessary under a shield of anonymity—you might care to write something about college realities and experience. I gather from what little Mr. Sherman has vouchsafed to tell me that you have watched occasional revolts of the spirit against the decorum of college life, and that these are matters on which you have your own opinions.

I cannot but wonder whether, in this transitional era of women's rights and activities, something of your experience with girls in college and women in the Faculty might not be interesting. At any rate, I trust you will not consider this letter too intrusive.

Yours sincerely,
Ellery Sedgwick

It was incredible—I couldn't believe my eyes! The distinguished editor of the *Atlantic Monthly* had actually invited me to write an article for the magazine. I floated on air, in a kind of intoxication. Soon all my worries would be over! I could resign my position, find a little home for Barbara and myself, and devote my full time to the thing I had always wanted to do—writing stories, articles, and books. It was such a dazzling prospect that I almost forgot to acknowledge Mr. Sedgwick's letter.

But, somehow, I couldn't sit down and start the piece. I was so surrounded by girls and women that I could not think of anything interesting to say about them. There were endless, logical excuses for delaying the fearful moment. It was far more fascinating just to contemplate my future as an author. Perhaps I could postpone it until after my summer in Norway and Sweden. Only recently word had come that I was to be one of the representatives from Colorado to the Conference of the International Federation of University Women, to be held in Christiania. The experience would broaden my outlook, I reasoned, and give me greater self-confidence. Then another note came from Mr. Sedgwick suggesting that he would like to use the article, if possible, in the June issue.

So, finally, I took myself in hand one night, sat at my desk with paper and pencil, prepared to start my career as an author. Immediately a kind of paralysis seized me. My thoughts had scattered like maple leaves in an autumn wind. I was conscious of Miss Loomis' ghostly figure hovering over me, waiting to censor every sentence, quick to remind me that I was a pretentious upstart, a threat to the prestige of the Dean of Women of Colorado College. I searched my mind for Patricia Thorne, forgetting that her abode was in the heart. I began to realize that I had no authentic ideas about the members of my own sex. Writing letters to Stuart Sherman was one thing, and superficial at that, but writing a paper for a national magazine required a skill and power of insight that I had not yet attained. I doubted if, in the early years of my marriage, I had ever shown a spark of talent for writing anything but the most rudimentary compositions, and now I was ready to give up in despair and recognize the truth.

But in some way I had to see it through, for better or for worse. It would be unthinkable to let Stuart Sherman down, without making an effort to fill Mr. Sedgwick's request. Night after night I labored over the difficult task and, at last, sent the manuscript to the *Atlantic Monthly*. The speed with which the piece was returned left me a bit dizzy, but there was a certain comfort to be squeezed from the editor's gracious, tactful rejection. "Someway or other it misses fire," he wrote. "It is good nervous writing, but the narrative does not tell a story that one instinctively remembers. Were I to pick up the paper, as any reader would, utterly without knowledge of its origin and growth, I should say, 'There's a woman who has thought about things, and to whom things have happened. She has a story to tell, but for some reason or other, she wants to soft-pedal it. She writes as if she expected someone to peek through the keyhole at any moment and catch her in the act.' The melancholy fact remains that your narrative is too discursive to catch and hold attention. That you could write a most interesting paper I am more sure of than ever, but what is still more present in my mind is the fact that I have intruded on your busy life and made it unnecessarily and uselessly busier."

A few days later, Stuart Sherman wrote as if to soften the blow.

> *By the way, do you ever see this whole business of life, the business of being a Dean of Women—or a Professor— as a "burning and shining light" to the young, through the tinted, crystalline of humor? I suspect you of desiring to see the spectacle as romance. I say, give it up. Try humor instead. One can include, perhaps, a little vein of romance in the humorous atmosphere. But humor is a much more durable garment than romance. It is for one thing, more capacious. Romance, comparatively speaking, is a skin-tight garment. But one can bring home groceries in the side pockets of the other——*

But I was not too discouraged by the *Atlantic's* rejection. Instead, I felt grateful to be relieved of an assignment for which I was unprepared. It was necessary for me to lengthen my perspective, to fight life less and love it more. It was going to be a number of years, and under very different circumstances, before I would be able to make the steep grade to Ellery Sedgwick's sanctum. But once the distant hope had been rekindled, I never lost sight of the goal.

VIII

I had planned to take Barbara with me on the Scandinavian journey. Our continued separations had worried me a great deal, and I felt guilty because of my apparent inability to provide a real home for us both. The long vacation together promised to give us a chance to catch up with each other and get better acquainted. But she had definite notions about what she wanted, and a whole summer spent abroad exclusively with her mother would have been "a waste of time." She was past fourteen now and had her heart set more than ever on work in the theater. I had begun to lean toward the permissive philosophy of progressive education and gave in to her tearful pleas to let her return to the Perry-Mansfield Camp. She waved wildly from the platform crowded with other happy campers, until the whistle blew and the train disappeared from sight. But there was a choke in my throat as I turned away, feeling that the chance to be with her might never come again. In another week I would be sailing on the SS *Gripsholm* not knowing that I was bound for one of the most momentous experiences of my career.

The train from Göteborg to Christiania teemed with women from some twenty different countries, with the notable exception of Germany. Although the war had been over for six years, hatred of the enemy lingered on, and German university women had not been invited to send representatives to the conference. The air vibrated with the confusion of tongues and smiling gestures speaking more eloquently than words. Strange, unpronounceable names no longer mattered; the shape or color of a face was as unimportant as the hairdo or the cut of a garment. A spirit of kinship seemed to move us all; we were human beings together suddenly released from the inhibiting fears and prejudices of our lives back home, wherever that home might be. It was as if we were discovering a new world of hope and fellowship; and peace was dawning on the horizon.

Among the 400 delegates, the largest number came from the United States; they were also the best dressed. We had emerged from the war rich, itinerant, and fired with faith in the League of Nations. The theme of the conference was "World Peace," and Fridtjof Nansen, the famous Norwegian arctic explorer and statesman, had been invited to make the key address. Sitting on the platform and in the audience, listening with rapt interest, were some of America's most distinguished women educators —Dean Virginia Gildersleeve of Barnard College; Bryn Mawr's M. Cary Thomas; Dean C. Mildred Thompson of Vassar; Mary E. Woolley, president of Mount Holyoke; Ellen Fitz Pendleton of Wellesley; and Bernice V. Brown, the beautiful young Dean of Radcliffe College.

But the Americans seemed to avoid each other to seek, instead, the friendship of women from alien countries, leaders like Christine Bonnevie, Norway's substitute member of the League of Nations; Countess Maria Loschi, the writer from Italy; Hedwig Kuranda, the scholarly philologist from the University of Vienna; and Caroline Spurgeon, economist from the University of London and president of the Federation. For me, however, the loveliest and most magnetic of all was Sweden's Annastina Alkman, a graduate of ancient Uppsala University, who lived in Göteborg and wrote feature articles for the *Göteborg Posten*, the city's most influential newspaper, published by her husband, Edvard Alkman.

She sat opposite me at the small table in the diner where I had gone for afternoon tea, on the way to Christiania. Her gracious manner drew me to her at once. She was very different from the stereotype of "excellent cooks and maids," which American women, including me, had come to think of as being Swedish. Reddish-gold hair waved softly over the ears and twisted in a knot at the back of her neck framed her face, and her eyes were as blue as the arctic midnight in June. She spoke English with a quaint, cultivated accent and we had no trouble understanding each other. When she joined me later in my compartment, I felt vaguely that I had known her someplace, a long time ago, and that we had merely picked up the thread of our friendship once again. I wondered if, perhaps, she might have a strain of American blood in her; she was so like some of our attractive women. She smiled when I told her this and said that her maternal forebears were Russian and her father was "pure Swede."

Our reservations were at the same hotel and soon we became inseparable companions, eating meals together, sitting side by side at the banquets, luncheons, and sight-seeing excursions. In the late evening, as her deadline neared, I went with her and waited while she telephoned the story of the day's events to the *Göteborg Posten*. Then we would stroll along the quiet boulevards, under the midsummer sky, and discuss the speakers we had heard and their inspiring points of view. "It was a great mistake," she said once, "not to invite the German University Women's Association to send delegates. What a strange contradiction that we should be talking of peace while we sowed seeds of resentment among our former enemies that might easily help increase the temper for another war."

More often we talked about the women of our two countries and how they differed in customs and outlook and temperament. "You Americans are so gay and free," she said, "your élan vital is very charming. It is because your sky is high and sunny; you are not shut in, like Swedes, by low skies and darkness much of the year. We are a melancholy, discontented people, with cranky dispositions, and often quick to flare up in anger."

"But we are imprisoned by other walls, no less desolating to the spirit," I said, "and perhaps our seeming gaiety is only a cover for our loneliness." I told her then about Barbara and our years together in Bemis Hall, and how I had been hoping to marry again and make a home. Instead, I had no alternative but to stay on in the college as a sort of official chaperon. She laughed when I recounted all the small rules and regulations I was expected to enforce and the many behavior problems with students I was unable to solve; and how I had gone running to the New York School of Social Work for the answers. "You must come back to Sweden," she said, "and here you will find a good Swedish husband and live happily ever after with your young daughter—I think you both would make very nice Swedes." Her face brightened suddenly, as if with a happy thought. "Edvard and I have a friend," she said, "a recent widower, and the only psychiatrist in all of Sweden. His name is Dr. Poul Bjerre and he lives in the country not far away from Stockholm—yes, when you return soon to our land, I shall see that you and Poul meet!" Poor Dr. Bjerre! What chance had he against two women conspiring to ensnare him!

The days and nights slipped by too quickly and, as the close of the conference approached, it was hard to think of saying good-by to Annastina. I had scheduled a ten-day tour of the Norwegian fiords, but, at her urging, canceled much of it in order to spend a little time with her, Edvard, and their eighteen-year-old daughter, Eva, at the farm a few miles from Göteborg, where they spent the summers.

The Alkmans had never owned an automobile; we took the train to the city to visit places of interest. The streets were wide and well-swept, mailboxes hung from the rear of the spotless blue and yellow trolley cars, and pots of flowering plants danced from the lampposts. Even the railroad station, set down in a beautiful garden with baskets of fuchsias and begonia fringing the eaves, added its touch of merriment to the scene. No signs of poverty or squalor could be seen anywhere to mar the impression of well-being. Instead of the usual slums which crowd the outskirts of large American cities, there were only colony gardens. Any worker could secure a tiny plot of ground for a trifling fee, build a shed according to his choice of city-approved models, just large enough to hold his tools, a cot, stove and table—in case he wished to spend the weekend cultivating flowers and vegetables for his family.

Edvard took special pride in showing me the harbor, alive with ships going to and coming from many world ports, filled mostly with pulp logs and iron from Lapland. "There is the SS *Gripsholm* just docking, from the United States," he said, pointing, "and when it returns you will be on it—unless we can persuade you to stay on with us and become a good Swedish citizen!" But for Edvard the most inspiring sight of all was the Art Museum, and I quickly caught his enthusiasm. Guarding the front entrance was Carl Milles' powerful sculpture, "The Poseidon Fountain." "I was the first to discover this gifted artist," Edvard said a bit boastingly, "and now you will see his magnificent fountains in Stockholm, Paris, the United States, and many other cities and countries. He is my close friend. When you come back to Sweden again, we shall go to Stockholm and you will meet him and Olga, his Austrian wife, and perhaps have tea with them at their villa at Lidingö." Then, inside, he pointed out the etchings of Anders Zorn, the paintings of Ernst Josephson—"they called him the mad artist"—the graceful bird and animal pictures of Bruno Liljefors; and the water colors of beloved Carl Larsson. "You will see his portrait of Annastina in our Göteborg home," he said; "when I die we shall give it to the National Art Museum in Stockholm."

On the last day, while Brita packed a basket of pastries and tinned delicacies for me to take on shipboard, we all went for a long walk in the woods to look for lingenberries and mushrooms for dinner. And that night we gathered in the living room to listen while Edvard read, in his deep, dramatic voice, *The Children of the Lord's Supper,* by Esais Tegner, Sweden's most noted nineteenth-century poet. I did not understand the words but I felt the rhythm and cadence of the lines and caught a sense of their meaning through Edvard's moving eloquence.

"Now," he said, when he had finished, "you shall go back another hundred years and hear the lyric poems of Carl Mikael Bellman, who improvised both words and music as he accompanied himself on a zither and strolled from tavern to tavern, singing his bacchanalian songs and living from the small coins tossed at his feet. When you are with us sometime in Stockholm, we shall take you for lunch at the barrel-shaped cellar called 'The Golden Peace,' where Bellman spent most of his time composing ribald verses and setting them to music as he went along." He said something in Swedish to Annastina and Eva and then turned to me. "Annastina thinks she can sing the songs and translate them at the same time, and Eva will accompany her on the piano. Now we shall see what kind of entertainment they can offer!"

All went well, if not too smoothly, for the first two or three songs. Then Edvard asked for his favorite, the one called "Ulla at the Window in Fishertown." "You take care of the verse, Stina," he said, "and I'll join in with the chorus." And she sang in a clear, sweet voice:

> "Ulla, mine Ulla, to thee may I proffer
> Reddest of strawberries, milk and wine,
> Or a bright carp from the fen shall I offer,
> Or but a bowl from the fountain so fine?
> Truly the flood-gates of heaven are broken——
> Rich is the scent of flower and tree——
> Drizzling, the clouds now the sun but foretoken,
> Thou may'st see."

The mood of the music changed with the gay, happy words of the chorus and Edvard's deep baritone boomed:

> "Isn't it delightful, little Fishertown?
> 'Delightful be it spoken.'
> Here the rows of tree-trunks stretching proudly down
> In brand-new gown;
> There the quiet reaches
> Of the inlet flow;
> And off yonder mid the ditches
> Ploughed land, lo!
> Isn't it delightful—all these meadows, though?
> 'Delightful, so
> Delightful, oh!'"

Annastina started off bravely with the second verse:

> "Hail, sweet, who there at the window dost hover!
> Hark how the bells from the city sound!
> See how the dust-clouds the carriages cover
> All the green hue——"

Then all of a sudden Edvard spoke out sharply, interrupting her. The music stopped and Eva sat frozen on the piano stool. A quick angry argument followed in Swedish, between the mother and father, which left me wondering what under the sun could have happened. Edvard's face grew red and apoplectic and Annastina answered back in her cool, quiet way. But in a few moments it was easy to see that she was beginning to give in to him, and then, as suddenly as it began, the quarrel ended. Eva started playing the piano again; Annastina finished the verse as if nothing had gone wrong; and Edvard sat back comfortably in his chair, basking in his victory.

"You and Edvard seemed to have had a disagreement last night," I said to Annastina the next morning. "Was it about the way you translated the songs?"

"Yes; and I was quite right."

"But apparently you gave up. An American woman would never have done that. If she feels that she is right, and sometimes even when she knows she isn't, she will defend her opinion to the bitter end."

"Ah, my dear friend," she replied, "we Swedish wives know that there are many more important things than winning an argument with one's husband."

I began to hope that Dr. Bjerre and I would never even meet, for no Swedish psychiatrist, I felt sure, would feel equal to coping with an American Dean of Women!

I arrived back in New York full of great anticipations. Stuart Sherman, his wife, Ruth, and son John about to enter Harvard were living on Jane Street in Greenwich Village, and they had invited me to dinner. It was our first meeting and I had the suspicion that Ruth had been a party to my literary escapade with her husband and knew me better than I realized. The thought made me self-conscious and ill at ease for a moment. But their simplicity and charm soon restored my composure.

Here again, as with Annastina, it seemed as though we had known each other always. Stuart was even handsomer than I had imagined, tall and dark with deep-set eyes, and his manner had a certain urbanity seldom found among professors I had known. I could not detect the least disappointing eccentricity about him—as I had fearfully expected—and realized that he had captured my heart as well as my mind.

John had an engagement for the evening, and Stuart, Ruth, and I sat in his book-lined study talking until long past midnight, when the coals in the fireplace had begun to cool. He spoke of the critical monograph he was doing on the works of Sinclair Lewis, and we drifted naturally into the absorbing subject of writing. He asked me if I had given up the idea of trying to become an author. I assured him that the hope never left me, but that I lacked faith in myself and questioned my talent.

"Why shouldn't you write?" he said, slowly puffing on his pipe. "You should. In veiw of Patricia's circumstances"—he still clung to the familiar name—"she should. If she has any good news, she should. If she wishes to escape from dungeons, she should. If she wishes to communicate with others in dungeons, she should. Once before I spoke of this when I thought Patricia was in a position to express her life by other means than words—which are, of course, only one poor dialect of the soul. But if that is not the case, then words, by all means."

"I remember it well—you said the important thing was to express—to 'externalize' whatever beauty one felt."

Ruth listened quietly, commenting occasionally as the conversation went on. But I was conscious of her quick, blue eyes observing me, as if trying to fathom the strange woman who had come into their lives little more than a year ago. Surely she had never known a Dean of Women like Patricia Thorne! Stuart reminded her that we had run out of coffee and suggested that she make a few sandwiches; and he got up to brace the dying fire with a bit of kindling and some boards from a broken crate left over from moving.

"Of course," he began again, after settling back in his big comfortable chair, "I've never experienced the torments of living in a women's dormitory, but one of your joyous nature should be able to accept the necessity gracefully. And I can give you a very good reason for *not* writing—gracefully." He looked into the snapping flames absently, as if speaking to himself. "The life of a person who lives by the pen is a daily hell and purgatory—with only the faintest glimpses of a better place. There is simply nothing in it unless you relish a grinding effort ninety-nine per cent of the time. That is my opinion. Also the opinion of *good* writers, better writers than myself. I began too late, so I think I know more of the effort than of the satisfactions of the pen. But even those who began at a fairly early age make copious expression of the tortures which are the daily lot of the conscientious penman."

He looked at me searchingly, as if to determine the effect of his jeremiad and his heart softened as he noted my dejection. "Don't let me discourage you too much," he said, "if you really have it in you—this compulsion to write—it will come out in spite of all the warnings of crotchety professors and disillusioned editors. By the way," he added, changing the subject, "I recently met the editor of *Good Housekeeping* magazine—Bigelow is his name—he has made a spectacular success of it. Somewhere he had got the idea that I might do a piece for him on why daughters hate their mothers, or something of the sort. The fee was dazzling—but it wasn't for me. It's more in your line. If you wish, I'll give you a card to him. You might possibly get together on an article."

I was fortunate in securing an appointment with Mr. Bigelow the next afternoon. For some reason, I expected the editor of

Good Housekeeping to be a fat, comfortable, homebody kind
of man. Instead, he was thin and angular except for the round
hump of his shoulders. His head, with its sparse graying hair,
was small and hard-looking, like a filbert. He listened with visible impatience while I explained the purpose of my call and
told something of my background and experience. Then, all of a
sudden, he thundered, "Why don't Deans of Women stay at
home and take care of their dormitories. Evidently that's no
longer the fashion—they must go traipsing about the country
and in the meantime the young people are going to the devil."

"You are paying the deans a great tribute," I said, "if you
think their mere presence in the dormitories would keep young
people from going to the devil. Personally, I could do a better
job living off campus where I could make some kind of acceptable home for my own daughter." I tried to tell him that the
position of Dean of Women was changing; that the old-style
moralists and disciplinarians were being displaced by counselors
trained in mental hygiene. "In a few years," I predicted boldly,
"no Deans of Women would be living 'in residence' and an
entirely different approach would be made in dealing with undergraduate problems." He seemed interested, all of a sudden,
and more attentive. "Why wouldn't that make a good subject
for an article?" I asked, surprised by my inventiveness.

"Not a bad idea," he said abruptly. "Try it out—see what you
can do with it." And then, as I was leaving, he added, "Come
in and see me whenever you're in New York—don't be scared
away by my bark. It's much worse than my bite."

I was in a state of euphoria all the way back to Colorado
Springs and could hardly wait for the week's holiday with Barbara to hear about the play at camp, in which she had the
leading role, and to tell her about my own exciting summer.

IX

It was a letdown to return to the campus with its weedy irrigation ditches and still, deserted buildings. The smell of freshly varnished furniture and waxed floors brought back my first depressing day in Bemis Hall. For a moment the old impulse to escape seized me. Oh, to fly away to Sweden once more and stroll in the woods with Annastina, Edvard, and Eva! Oh, the endless camps and boarding schools —why was I always having to say good-by to Barbara! Nothing, it seemed, nothing that I longed for most had been realized.

In spite of everything that had been done to make it so, the apartment had never felt like home. Jessie, as usual, had it in readiness. The shades had been drawn just right, so as to shut out the bright sun and let in the wonderful view of the mountains; the books and pictures had been carefully dusted; autumn asters were in the Van Briggle vase on the desk. But only Jessie herself gave me a sense of familiarity and warmth, and as I heard her hurrying down the corridor to my living room, my spirits lifted and exhilaration began to return, but not for long.

"That girl"—she always spoke of Penny as 'that girl'—"came early again this year. I put her in the guest room, as I thought you'd want me to, and kept a watch on her. That fella, Tony, she goes with has been hanging 'round day and night. I declare, it'll be a blessing when she's gone for good——"

Although she was bright, Penny had never reached her full capacity as a student. But with my prodding, now and then, and closing my eyes to most of her peccadilloes, she finally came to the last leg of the perilous journey toward an A.B. degree. The prospect was heartening. In some way, my own success or failure seemed to hinge on her graduation from college. In my moments of truth, however, it had to be admitted that I had never penetrated her shell of defiance. Occasionally, when we met on campus or in the dormitory, she would stop long enough for me to ask news of her parents—her father's other wife had had a baby girl, and her mother was leaving soon on another long trip. "She hasn't found a husband yet" was the usual laconic comment.

Soon again I was caught up in the opening events of the college year, and Penny no longer hovered on the rim of my conscience. She was a senior now and I could let go of her. But my reckoning was premature. She still had a trump card up her sleeve!

It was just after the Christmas holidays. I was sitting at my desk, late one night, trying to make an outline of the article for *Good Housekeeping* magazine. For some reason, all my brilliant ideas had become hazy; the sentences would not stick together. It was increasingly evident that I was not equipped with enough knowledge or experience to attempt such a piece. What I actually wanted to write about was the Dean as a human being, but these thoughts were hidden deep in my secret garden and I was not yet ready to expose them to the full light. Again I would have to shut the window on an opportunity that Stuart Sherman had thrown my way. The grim truth would have to be faced, I confessed, brushing off a sorrowful tear; I was never meant to be a writer——

All of a sudden there was a timid knocking on my open door and I looked up to see Penny, of all people, leaning wearily against the frame. "May I come in?" she asked. "It's terribly late and I hate to bother you but I couldn't go to sleep —maybe it will help to talk with you."

Never before in almost four years had she sought me out of her own free will. Her face was pale and drawn and her eyes were red from weeping. "Of course, come in—what under the sun has happened, Penny?"

She was direct, as usual.

"You won't want me around when I tell you—you see, I'm going to have a baby——"

"Oh my dear——" The breath caught in my throat and then Dr. Ebaugh's words flashed back: listen and never be shocked; another person's confidence is one of the most precious things in life.

"When did it happen?"

"Oh, it's not what you think—that I'm not married. Tony and I eloped to Golden last Labor Day. I have the certificate right here," she held out a crumpled piece of paper, "the Justice of the Peace gave it to us—Tony told me to show it to you in case——"

"That isn't necessary; I believe you."

"We knew that it was against the college rules but we were desperately in love and thought we could keep the secret until after Commencement. But the baby—it is four months now and I can't hide it much longer—already some of the girls suspect. I've been worried to death about what to do." She wiped her eyes and struggled for control. "Please understand, Dean Lee, I know I don't deserve it and I'm willing to take any punishment—throw me out of the dorm, if you want to—but just don't let them fire Tony. He's studying to be a doctor and if he has to quit college without a degree, he'll never get into medical school—please—please don't let the faculty expel him —we didn't do anything wrong——"

"I wouldn't say that," I replied, "you and Tony did a very impulsive thing, involving a grave responsibility. You also realized that you were violating a long-standing regulation against the marriage of students while in college. I don't know what action the faculty will take. I am only one member but I shall do what I can to help you and Tony through this trouble. Meanwhile, it is better not to discuss the matter with others until I can get in touch with your mother——"

"No, not *her*," she interrupted, with a trace of the old bitterness, "my father is the one. I'll write him myself tonight."

In spite of precautions, the news of the elopement leaked out, and soon the whole campus was buzzing with gossip and speculation. Tony had been the season's popular football star and was a likely candidate for Phi Beta Kappa. Undergraduates lined up ready to fight for him. It was time, they said, for Colorado College to shake off a few moth-eaten traditions and get in step with other institutions. *The Tiger*, the student paper, pointed out that the state university had been permitting married students to live on campus ever since the end of the war, that former barracks had been made into apartments for their use, and nursery schools were being established for their children. "Why all this squeamishness," one heated editorial read, "about pregnant women pursuing their studies and mingling with others in the classrooms? Is motherhood so degrading that it must be banished from the ivory tower of higher education?"

But in faculty meetings the tone was more conservative. When a young man married, it was claimed, he should go to work and support his wife and family. This was an obligation that prevailed among civilized people in our country. Furthermore, for reasons of health, a woman should be sheltered at home during her pregnancy. It did not look well for her to mix with other less experienced, unmarried girls. But the younger instructors were quick to protest such a point of view. Marriage, they argued, with its settling influence, would improve the scholarship of those concerned, and nobody's morals would be contaminated by daily association with a girl in the family way. Finally, the faculty voted for the appointment of a committee to consider the problem and to accept its recommendations.

Penny's father arrived from New York on the first train, prepared, he announced, to stand by his daughter "to the bitter end." And Tony's parents drove up from the little New Mexican village where the father was pastor of the Community Church. The faculty committee met with them in my living room to determine what could be done. Both families were fiercely loyal to their errant son and daughter and agreed to help them find a small house in town and pledged their support if the college would waive its rule and permit Tony to be graduated with his class. The committee, which was made up of the younger teachers and administrators, went even further and urged that the faculty settle the issue with dignity and magnanimity by allowing both students to continue their courses and receive degrees "in absentia, if necessary,"—a comment that relieved tension and filled the room with approving laughter.

The affair marked a milestone in liberalizing college policies regarding married students. The storm that raged around Tony and Penny soon faded in importance. No one looked twice, that June, at the young senior sitting on the curbing in front of Coburn Library holding hands with his expectant wife while she quizzed him on Gray's *Anatomy*. No one, that is, but Jessie when she happened to be passing by. "That girl," I once heard her mutter, "she never did Colorado College any good—Miss Loomis would have sent her packing instanter, that very first day!" Then she sighed and hurried away down the hall. "I declare," she often mumbled to herself (as time passed she talked more and more to herself), "I don't know what young folks are coming to!"

Dear, conscientious Jessie! She was fighting a losing battle against the encroaching future!

Problems of human behavior grew more complicated as I became more aware of them. The old formulas satisfied Jessie and her generation but they were totally inadequate for modern situations. Rules alone were not the answer. They had a tendency to pyramid and topple over from weariness and sometimes made the college authorities appear witless and a bit ridiculous. Cigarette smoking, for instance, was now permitted only in the privacy of a girl's room "on condition that she provide a metal wastebasket." The threat of fire was great but, at best, indulgence in tobacco had been removed from the category of morals. The same could not be said about liquor. The Volstead Act was making a travesty of all law. Homemade gin flowed in such abundance and secrecy that trying to check it was like using a coal shovel to stop the leaks in a spilling dam.

But the college still clung to its regulations, and the longer the list, the more secure everybody seemed to feel, especially the parents. Even if the world were going to the dogs, the mere statement in the annual catalogue that "the Dean of Women lived in residence" sounded a reassuring note that all was well with the girls. But they themselves were not deceived and often must have caught ironical glimpses of the Dean's own feet of clay.

My need of further study in psychology was urgent, not for just a summer's term but for a long year of work. I began pondering the idea of going to the New School for Social Research in New York where Alfred Adler, the famous Austrian psychiatrist, was lecturing on "Individual Psychology," and the keen intellect of Everett Dean Martin was throwing new light on the erratic behavior of crowds. The longer I dwelt on the prospect the more I rationalized it. Miss Crouch could take over my duties as Acting Dean. Such an experience would enable me to visit again some of the leading eastern colleges for women and renew my acquaintance with Dean Brown, at Radcliffe, whom I came to know and like at the conference in Christiania. Also, I had been dissatisfied with Barbara's school and had been considering, for some time, sending her east to one of the fine boarding schools in Connecticut but dreaded putting such a wide distance between us. If I were in New York, she could come there for vacations and take in some of the great music and plays. And then—a very powerful incentive —for good companionship occasionally there would be Stuart and Ruth Sherman. The cost made me hesitate and do some figuring. If Barbara and I spent the summer in my Bemis Hall apartment, I could afford the expense, with something left over. Fortunately, a small inheritance from an old friend would take care of her year's tuition.

I was on the verge of writing the Shermans one of my most joyous letters when a troubled note came from Stuart, saying that he had had to take his son out of Harvard and put him in Cragmor, the sanitarium for tuberculous patients in Colorado Springs. He wondered if I would be so kind as to buy him a large bowl of goldfish, "something to rest his eyes on now and then—I'm doing my best to keep him contented there." I had a wonderful time selecting six or seven brightly colored fish, together with a tower and all the food and plant life they required, and taking them out to John. It was reward enough to see the pleased smile on his face, but an extra dividend came a week later in a charming letter from Stuart. It read,

Dear Patricia:
    You executed the mission in a most masterly way—not merely executed it successfully but with art and triumph. I refer to the selections of distinguished and distinguishable individuals among the fish rabble, the selection of the central

*tower, the bowl, the crab-meat. And more than that, you went
yourself and appeared on the threshold like a Fairy Princess,
thus making the day into an event at Cragmor. And more
than that you wrote about your visit delightfully, and about
your "adventure" in the discovery of the fish. To give the
final touch of grace, you liked John—or spoke, at least, as
if you thought him a likeable boy——But I don't so much
credit you for liking him, you understand, as for saying so.
In the same mail with your letter came one from him describing the event! So we had the thing four square. He was
delighted—included a pen drawing of the largest fish, so that
we should appreciate his, or her, configurations. Between the
two of you—both capital letter writers—the morning was
gay.*

> *Very gratefully yours,*
> *Stuart Sherman*

He then added a postscript saying that there was a possibility
of his lecturing at the Colorado College Summer School. "Please
let us know of any house that might accommodate itself to my
invalid son, his extremely busy father, and a mother who is
doing her best to make us all comfortable and happy." Their
coming in a few weeks filled me with excitement. It would make
the empty shell of Bemis Hall less isolated and lonely. I looked
forward to hikes over canyon trails with Ruth and Barbara and
evenings with the whole family when Stuart would read aloud
to John. And then, of course, I would attend the lectures ten
hours a week.

As it turned out, I saw very little of him. In addition to the
college courses, he continued his weekly articles for the *Herald
Tribune*, often reading as many as twenty books in preparation
for a single piece. His working hours lasted from nine in the
morning until twelve or one o'clock at night, and his day off

was spent in rewriting and again rewriting the story for the week. It was a terrible physical and nervous strain, but he was occupying a unique position in the country's journalism as the man who could produce a first-rate critical article for his paper every Sunday. But he never complained of the load and seemed as pleased as any artist with what he had done well.

When Summer School closed, John returned to Cragmor and Stuart and Ruth went to their cabin at Dunewood on the shores of Lake Michigan where they had always spent their university holidays. One afternoon, in late August, they pushed off in their canoe against a strong surf. Suddenly the canoe capsized and they started to swim ashore. Both were very much at home in the water and making good headway when Ruth shrieked to some campers on shore that she could not see Stuart. The water was only four feet deep and men lifted him from the bottom and carried him to the beach. They worked over him for more than an hour, but his heart had snapped. Stuart Sherman, at age forty-five, was dead.

In one of his last letters to John he wrote:

You have asked me how to live: that happens in my opinion to be the most important and the most neglected of all studies among the American people—how to live so that life shall taste somehow good each day as it passes here on earth. . . . At the end of the dusty trails upon which we gallop so hard and hot, at the top of the difficult ascents to which we climb by perilous finger and toe holds, there is nothing better than these fruits of the contemplative life—time to cultivate the fine arts; music, art, literature, conversation, friendship, reflection, and a personal philosophy. . . . Now in the quiet cubicles of Cragmor I heard nothing but wit and philosophy. I came away after each visit with a clearer vision of the way to live.

Carl Van Doren, his close friend and former colleague, wrote: "Somewhere in him was a greatness not to be measured." And something had vanished from my life that had imparted a glow to it, an animation and a charm that never could be replaced.

X

I learned from Stuart Sherman how to mine the deep riches of the mind but it was Ruth, his widow, who taught me how to pick up the pieces of a broken life and mend them with courage. She returned to the big empty house on Jane Street and immediately sought work of some kind to occupy her time. It was not difficult for a woman of her competence. She had been graduated from Vassar College with honors in chemistry and mathematics and easily qualified as a reader with a large firm publishing textbooks in New York City. I was delighted when she offered to let me rent Stuart's study during my stay. It was a commodious room with a daybed for me and a couch for Barbara whenever she had vacations.

The New School was everything I had expected and I looked forward, enthusiastically, to a year of rewarding studies and lectures. My notebooks were filled with ideas to put into practice when I returned to Bemis Hall. I had begun to see football rallies, blanket tossings, fraternity serenades, and shirttail parades as phenomena of crowd behavior; and they became less frightening, even amusing.

I examined myself with devastating honesty and questioned whether I actually wanted to marry and settle down again. I had become too discriminating. Perhaps I had inherited my prospector father's roving nature; and the smell of fresh earth and the lure of distant mountains had become part of my marrow. Could it be, I asked myself, that I had never really grownup but was still a romantic young girl, only a few years removed from the students I was trying to help and understand? And what about Barbara—why had I been unable or unwilling to make a home for her—was I truly lacking in the maternal instinct? These and many other thoughts haunted me during the self-searching hours in the dark of the night. "The individual grows mature," Alfred Adler had said, "by facing and accepting mature situations."

But zeal for learning and a driving curiosity about life kept me from becoming too morose about situations that, at the moment, couldn't be helped. Here and there I was finding cracks in New York's hard-boiled exterior and to lose my fear of it. When Miss Maude Wetmore, president of the Women's Civic Federation, invited me to speak at one of the large monthly dinners at the Colony Club, I accepted without hesitation. This was a powerful organization of social leaders whose purpose was to get behind the men in promoting good works for the city. My subject was "Why Come East?" which left me ample room for saying almost anything that came to mind; and it surprised even myself that I was able to describe the Dean's work as a highly amusing experience and to illustrate it with humorous anecdotes.

Other speakers were the dynamic Anne Morgan, whose important project at the moment was in helping to build a magnificent new club for the American Woman's Association, whose membership was composed of prominent business and professional women. She was followed by Mrs. Otis Skinner, lovely, dark-haired wife of the distinguished actor, who told of the joys and worries of bringing up Cornelia, her stage-struck young daughter, and advised other mothers not to despair, that a love of acting was a phase through which most adolescent girls passed, and that only time would tell if the talent were genuine. Sitting next to me was Anne Parrish, formerly of Colorado Springs and now a successful novelist. She was slender, blonde, and pretty, and spoke engagingly of the delights and perils of being a writer. I was naturally drawn to her, not only because of her charming wit and the fact that we had a few friends and acquaintances in common but because of my undying interest in writing. She won my heart at once by commenting that I had the flavor of the West in my manner—the West that she had known as a child—and that I should try to write about it. When the evening came to a reluctant end, she invited me to tea with her the next afternoon.

If I had fully realized the extent of wealth, social prestige, and fame represented there, I never would have had the temerity to stand up before such a gathering and speak my cavalier piece. But I was carried along by a sort of infectious excitement and by the sheer wonder of life. It was only long afterward when I had grown in wisdom and sophistication that the recollection of my naïveté gave me shivers of stage fright and chagrin.

The winter's high point was reached when Barbara joined me for the Christmas holidays. We lined up outside the Metropolitan Opera House, for standing room on the inside, to hear Chaliapin sing in *Boris Godunov*. We climbed to the topmost balcony at the Playhouse to see Jane Cowl in *The Road to Rome* and shed copious tears over the tragedy of Helen Hayes in *Coquette*, at the Maxine Elliott. Our weary feet led us through the maze of the Public Library and we lingered, spellbound, gazing at the priceless masterpieces in the Metropolitan Museum of Art.

With the coming of spring, an unexpected event cut short my year at the New School. A letter arrived one day from Mr. G. Hilmar Lundbeck, head of the Swedish Steamship Company, saying that his friends, the Edvard Alkmans, had suggested that I might be interested in making some talks about Sweden, its people, scenic beauty, and places of historical importance, in the western part of the United States where I lived. His company, he went on, was anxious to attract more tourists and to create a better understanding of the country's cultural life. He regretted that he could not offer me an honorarium for such services, but said that I would be given first-class passage on one of the newest Swedish liners, as well as transportation on the Swedish National Railways to cities in Sweden which I might wish to visit. Furthermore, I would be supplied with books and other materials, such as colored slides, as preparation for the talks.

I wrote him that I would leave on the SS *Kungsholm* in ten days. It was mid-April and I figured that I might stay two months, returning in time to spend the summer with Barbara. But the gods did not will it that way. Shortly after the Lundbeck letter reached me, another came from Mr. Philip Chase, director of the Harvard Summer School, saying that Dean Bernice Brown of Radcliffe College had suggested that I might consider the summer school's newly created position as Adviser to Women. It would require me to live in McClintock Hall, down by the Charles River, to have general supervision of all the women students and work with the several hall mistresses. The remuneration for the six weeks, starting July 5, would be $300 and room and board.

I shrank at the thought of spending the summer living in still another dormitory! But it struck me that something better might develop out of it, even some kind of position at Radcliffe that would enable me to see Barbara oftener. I had come to have great respect for this college and in my balmy moments dreamed that one day I would be connected with it in some capacity. I wanted it, I think, more than anything else for the settling-down phase of my career. So I accepted the Harvard offer, arranged for Barbara to attend the camp of an old friend over in New Jersey and set sail, with a free mind and happy anticipations, for two months in Sweden.

The past year had been a time of change for the Alkmans. Eva was in her first term at Uppsala University, and Edvard, had been elected to Parliament. He and Annastina had taken an apartment in one of the quaint gabled houses in Old Town, often called "the City Between the Bridges," which was founded in the 1220s by Birger Jarl. They had engaged a room for me near-by, together with a maid to fix my breakfast and a view that rivaled in grandeur the sweep of Pike's Peak and the Rampart Range from the picture window in Bemis Hall. Just around the corner was the Storkyrkan, the church where all the coronations since 1740 had taken place. In a nook bordering a leafy canal, the ancient Riddarhuset (House of Nobles) rested in quiet dignity. Across the Norrbro, the main bridge connecting the island with the modern city, I could see the Royal Opera House, the Grand Hotel, and, farther away, on still another island, the famous Town Hall designed by Ragnar Östberg. But these glimpses were merely a foretaste of what Annastina and Edvard had planned for the Swedish part of my *wanderjahr*.

As May began to unfold and touch shrubs and trees in the parks with tender green, Lake Mälaren, too, came alive with color. Hundreds of brightly colored little boats, freshly painted and refurbished, bobbed in the sparkling blue water; and along the Strandvägen, busy gardeners were mending the baskets that hung from the lampposts and filling them with spring and summer flowers. Although Edvard was a member of Parliament, and still owned and published the *Göteborg Posten,* and Annastina wrote feature stories for *Dagens Nyheter,* one of Stockholm's leading newspapers, motor cars were still a luxury, and, besides, they preferred walking and often spent their holidays on

long, cross-country jaunts. But they spared me from such un-
accustomed exercise and we went, instead, on picnics in the
wooded Djurgården, one of the archipelago's largest islands,
and strolled through the open-air Museum of Skansen to stay
on in the evening and watch the spirited folk dancers from
Skåne or Darlarna.

One afternoon Edvard hurried home to tell us to pack some
overnight things quickly. "We have a great treat in store," he
said, his face flushed with excitement. "Professor Fehr has invited us all to go sailing with him on his yacht"; then, in an
aside to me, "it was formerly owned by Anders Zorn, the noted
painter."

"Oh, how nice!" The sparkle in Annastina's eyes made it
plain that she had never expected such an unusual opportunity for me to see the Stockholm archipelago in its full vernal
beauty and to spend a night in one of the most charming summer homes on the east coast.

"Professor Fehr is a man of many talents, as well as wealth,"
Edvard went on. "He is not only a senator in the First Chamber
but a lawyer and a professor in the High School of Com-
merce——"

"And he is also a bachelor——" Annastina added, giving me
one of her matchmaking smiles.

It was my first outing on a yacht and I lounged on deck enchanted, dreaming through the quiet channels, out among the
emerald islands that studded the Baltic Sea. Sometimes the sails
of the little vessel barely missed the overhanging branches of
birch and willow and sent flocks of birds beating their wings in
the misty sky. Now and then we saw a landing pier and a tiny
blue and yellow canoe bobbed in the water as we passed; and
high above, half-hidden by treetops, a white cottage could be
glimpsed with a thin ribbon of smoke curling from the chimney.

I watched through dozing eyes as the long fingers of our skipper maneuvered the sails to catch the slightest breeze, the same fingers which, after dinner at the farm, would improvise delightful music, speaking to us in a common language with more meaning than human words could express.

The Alkmans found their recreation among literary and artistic men and women and they had arranged for me to meet and know some of the most celebrated. There was Ragnar Östberg, for instance, the hearty, engaging architect of Stockholm's well-known Town Hall. At a housewarming one evening, when we were going through the Swedish ceremony of calling each other by our given names, he laughed at my clumsy attempts to pronounce "Ragnar." "Oh," he teased, "just call me 'The Fox' for I am a very sly fellow of whom attractive ladies from America should beware!" He was scheduled to lecture during the winter months at the University of Michigan, and when I asked him what his style of architecture was called, he smiled and said self-confidently, "Let the professors decide that a hundred years hence!"

The women of Sweden, especially, fascinated me. Combining marriage and careers had long been an accepted way of life for them. They were leaders in politics and community welfare while their American sisters were still testing their strength. Their power pushed through laws for the protection of children born out of wedlock, for the improvement of conditions for workers in industry and better housing for low-income groups. It was Anna Lindhagan, sister of Stockholm's burgomaster, who founded Sweden's far-flung Colony Gardens. And Dr. Alma Sundquist who developed the successful program of sex education in the schools. Then, at a memorable luncheon at the Riksdag Restaurant, Kerstin Hesselgren, herself a member of Parliament, spoke to me about women in political life.

*She was a woman of about sixty [I wrote in my journal],
with silky grey hair combed back loosely from her forehead
and twisted in a coil at the neck. I asked about the use in
Sweden of Mental Hygiene in school or college counseling,
or in dealing with personnel problems in factories. "We in
this country are slow to accept the principles of modern psychology," she said, "it is as yet, too experimental. We shall
leave it to your young America to try it first and then we shall
follow someday, perhaps, and adopt what you have found
best—and so, we shall avoid some of your mistakes! Certainly,
Mental Hygiene and its techniques have not spread from the
hospitals and juvenile courts, to the schools and universities
of our country."*

When Selma Lagerlöf came to Stockholm for a few days from
her home in Mårbacka, Annastina invited her to tea. The purpose of her trip was to confer about a production of the new
Swedish opera *Gösta Berling,* based on her novel of the same
name, which was going to be produced at the Royal Opera
House in November in celebration of her seventieth birthday.
Annastina had briefed me, beforehand, about some of her remarkable achievements. In 1904 the Swedish Academy awarded
her the great Gold Medal. The University of Uppsala honored
her with the degree of Doctor of Literature in 1907; and in 1909
she received the Nobel Prize. Five years later she became the
first woman ever to be elected to the Swedish Academy.

I had read her two most famous books, *The Saga of Gösta
Berling,* and the children's classic used as a primary textbook in
the Swedish schools, *The Wonderful Adventures of Nils.* For
some reason I expected to find the author a remote, dignified
individual on the order of Ellen Fitz Pendleton, president of
Wellesley College. But I was in for a pleasant surprise.

She is a sweet, grandmotherly old lady [I wrote Barbara], with a calm, unwrinkled face and keen grey eyes. Her manner is shy and reserved, due perhaps to her frail childhood, or possibly to her years as a school teacher. She seems better suited to sitting in a rocking chair, reading her folk stories to the neighborhood children, than occupying a seat of honor in the renowned Swedish Academy. The severity of her black dress was relieved only by a double strand of shell pearls at the neck and a beautiful old brooch on her full bosom. Her fingers were laden with rings, thin, worn-looking gold bands, some with small settings of garnet, turquoise or opal. Surely they must have weathered most of the long years of her life!

In spite of Edvard's attempt to monopolize the conversation plying her with questions and giving suggestions for the direction of the *Gösta Berling* opera, the talk soon turned to books. She was better read than I in modern American fiction, and I was embarrassed when she asked who were considered the leading American novelists. For a moment, my mind went blank and I wished that Stuart Sherman might have been hovering near to whisper in my ear. Finally I mentioned offhand such writers as Thornton Wilder, Willa Cather, Ernest Hemingway, Edith Wharton——

"But you have omitted your most outstanding author," she said half-reprovingly, "an artist who is held in the highest regard in Europe——"

"Who is that?" I asked, trying to remember.

"Sinclair Lewis—he has given us a true picture of the life and people in the United States today. In *Main Street*, for instance, and *Babbitt*—none of your novelists today can equal him in the portrayal of American character——"

"But we do not believe that he gives a wholly honest picture," I said rather weakly, "he paints only the ugliness of our small towns and the tawdry side of people. He overlooks the beautiful and noble."

"Oh my dear," she said, as if I were one of her pupils of long ago, "you must understand that one cannot write of the ugly places, or the tawdry human beings that dwell in them, without first seeing them, as you say, 'beautiful and noble.' Lewis is one of your country's great idealists; indeed, he has the universal mark of genius."

Her words came back to me vividly two years later, in 1930, when Sinclair Lewis was awarded the Nobel Prize for Literature.

If Edvard felt cheated in his dominant role as host to Selma Lagerlöf, it was made up to him in our visit to the mansion of Prince Eugen, a younger brother of King Gustav V. He was not only a distinguished painter himself, but his collection of old masterpieces, foreign as well as native, was one of the finest in Sweden. Edvard was completely at home as our royal host led us through his gallery and told something of the history of the various works of art. My favorite among them all was a huge canvas covering most of one wall, called *Näcken*, painted by the "mad" Swede, Ernst Josephson. It pictured the folk tale of the youth, *Näcken*, bare-limbed and playing his violin, making melancholy music beneath a waterfall, enticing the beautiful maiden above to leap into his arms—and death. Because Josephson was believed to be insane, the government, many years before, had refused to accept Prince Eugen's offer to give the painting to the National Museum of Art. "Now," he said, with a complaisant smile, "the government has changed its mind— and so has Prince Eugen!"

The visit to Prince Eugen's gallery was followed, a few days later, by luncheon with Carl Milles and his wife, Olga. Edvard had been the first art critic to bring Milles' work to public attention, and ever since the two families had been close friends.

The Milles' villa in Lidingö, a suburb of Stockholm, stood on a
high hill with a sweeping view of the city, its lake and river and
many islands. It was surrounded by courtyards, terraces, and
sunken gardens, overlooked by Milles' famous heroic statue in
bronze, "The Sun Singer." He and Olga, also an artist, had
filled the rambling old house with their own beautiful creations,
in oil, metal, wood, alabaster, and marble. It had been his plan
to give it to the city as a center of intellectual and artistic life,
on condition that he and Olga could stay on there for the rest
of their days under a sort of subsidy. But there was considerable
opposition to the idea. Because a man could carve enormous
fountains in stone, it was argued, the city was not justified in
endowing him financially. And that day Milles revealed to Edvard that he was considering going to the United States in a
year or so to join the Scandinavian art colony which Eliel and
Loja Saarinen were developing at Cranbrook, near Detroit.

I was the object of much teasing after the Milles luncheon
because of my fondness for Olga's chocolate drops filled with
liqueurs. I had never tasted such sweets before and found them
delectable. "What will your students think of you," Edvard said,
when he saw that I had finished the last of the candy, "*you*,
citizen in the land of Prohibition returning home from Sweden
an alcoholic!" And, alas, home was not too far away!

The days and weeks rushed by and I was sadly aware that the
end of my Swedish holiday was in sight. All too soon I would
be roughing it in a bare dormitory at the Harvard Summer
School, devising rules of conduct for hundreds of women students, with as many different backgrounds and aims, ranging in
age from sixteen to sixty; and I tried to forget the unhappy
prospect!

It seemed as if there would not be time enough to go to
Uppsala the last of May to see the Commencement ceremonies,
but I was particularly anxious to share this experience with the

undergraduates at Colorado College and managed to make the trip. The Swedish university system, like that of other European schools and universities, differed essentially from that in America. Students completing the requirements for the bachelor's or master's degree simply departed for home with only a little certificate to show for their work. No graduating exercises livened the day, no proud parents were on hand to receive and offer congratulations, and no alumni came together to renew their youth in class reunions.

But when a candidate came up for his doctorate—it may have taken him as long as eight or ten years to do it—the whole country seemed to turn out in rejoicing. The burgomaster, provincial governor, and representatives from all of Sweden's twenty-four provinces, dressed in colorful regalia, marched in dignified procession while bands played and cannon boomed. The promoter, a professor chosen annually for the honor, read a learned paper in Latin about his researches with fifteen generations of flies, and the archbishop and chancellor sat in stiff splendor in blue plush chairs just below the podium. No applause marked the proceedings, nor singing either at the beginning or the end.

Afterward, Annastina and I went to visit two of the student clubs or "Nations" to which all undergraduates coming from the same provinces automatically belonged. In comparison, the American fraternity system struck the Swedes as being extremely undemocratic and even cruel in the practice of social discrimination. In some of the "Nations" there were a few sleeping rooms, but mostly they were recreation centers for both men and women. I was amazed to hear that no chaperons or "housemothers" were provided and when I asked Annastina about the need of supervision and what kept the young people from misconduct, she said: "Family pride. We are a homogeneous country, of one religion and race, except for our Laplanders, and our children are imbued with a strong sense of family loyalty and self-respect. Parents consider them grownup when they reach university age and let go of them to mature in their own way."

"But we have heard stories, in the United States, about the immorality that exists among the youth of Sweden. Is there no truth in them?"

"A bit, perhaps, among farm boys and girls who may have different customs, but they are not immoral according to your definition. Often they cannot marry because of the scarcity of land for starting new farms. Or they lack the money to support their own homes and must continue to live with their families. Meanwhile, the young people become 'engaged' and their relationship is understood and accepted."

"But if babies come," I said, "and marriage is still not possible——"

"They are given their father's name and he must support and educate them. That is the law that Kerstin Hesselgren helped fight for—and won. There is no such thing in Sweden as an illegitimate child, even though born out of wedlock. All alike must have the same opportunity to grow up as good Swedish citizens."

Perhaps it was because she thought better of it, and had given me up as a likely candidate for a Swedish husband, that our visit with Dr. Poul Bjerre, the psychiatrist, was saved until the last. He lived near the village of Tumba, a short train trip from Stockholm, on a wooded point of land that jutted into a small lake. A screen of fir and birch trees shielded the white farm buildings from the road. Like all the other Swedes I had come to know, he, too, had an avocation—painting and sculpture. His home was full of pictures by such artist friends as Carl Larsson, Anders Zorn, and Bruno Liljefors. On the newel post of the stairway stood a bronze head of Dr. Bjerre, the work of Carl Milles some twenty years before. All about the rooms, in lovely frames and hanging on the walls, were portraits in oil and water color of his dead wife. Surely he had no interest yet in choosing her successor!

He was a delightful host, with many amusing stories, and quick to catch the point of my own American humor, which often baffled the Swedes. While we were having lunch outdoors on the lawn, he talked interestingly of his psychological theories. "Because of them," he laughed, "I am frequently called crazy."

Recently, he said, he had published a book called *Death and Renewal,* which summed up his psychological credo of twenty years. He spoke of his conviction that all of existence is a continuous dying and coming to life again, and that there is no such thing as final death. "But Sweden," he went on, "is poor soil for the growth of psychological theories. Except for the hospitals for the insane, a psychiatrist might starve to death."

"Is it because your country is such a contented land?" I ventured.

"Exactly. It is thwarted and spiritually hungry people who seek a solution to their problems through psychoanalysis. Sweden is not marked by sharp conflicts in politics, religion, or social life. We are a conventional people, satisfied to observe accepted forms in conduct. Nations as well as individuals grow by their differences and learn from their conflicts. Sweden is on the way toward becoming Utopia, only to find that there is nothing left to struggle for—and the people have become soothed to unconsciousness."

"But you are regarded, now, as one of the most progressive and civilized countries in the world," I protested. "In the United States, we are years behind you in our social development. We are still torn with dissension and neurotic frustration—and screaming for the help of psychiatrists, and there are not enough to go around."

"Perhaps, Dr. Poul, you had better follow Milles' idea," Annastina said, "and emigrate to America——"

He smiled rather wistfully. "It is too late," he said, "and I myself am a contradiction of my own conclusions. This is home to me, the lake, the old trees, the garden—the peace. Long since, I have become narcotized by Sweden!"

I had been there less than three months and already had fallen under its spell. If Dr. Bjerre's thesis were true, that "all of life is a continuous dying and renewal," I hoped that when my own death came I might be reborn in this lovely land.

XI

Bemis Hall seemed to have lost many of its depressing aspects during my year away, or else I had grown less sensitive to them. It was a picture of warmth and appeal compared with the bare, austere rooms of McClintock Hall at Harvard University where I had spent most of the summer. The ghost of Miss Loomis no longer shadowed me, and the perennial urge to escape had vanished. For the first time, I felt at home. The irritating click of high heels running through the corridors and the girlish screams of laughter had become more subdued. The inevitable problems of student behavior that lay ahead appeared in the light of a challenge. Now they could be faced with confidence. Fear and insecurity no longer had power over me. I could bring something of value to the undergraduates, something learned from the inspiring teachers at the New School, and much of what I had seen and experienced in Sweden.

I saw the orientation of freshman girls, for instance, as an opportunity not only to acquaint them with campus traditions but to deepen their self-understanding. The stereotyped custom of packing them in together at one big meeting was discarded, and instead small groups were invited to Ticknor Study, where some of the younger faculty members gave talks on coming to know ourselves through literature, science, and the arts. Afterward, they came to my living room for tea and an hour of discussion and questions. And nowhere was any mention made of rules and regulations, and penalties. This distasteful duty had been turned over to the newly organized students' self-government board for the dormitories.

As it developed, the different emphasis educated me even more than it did the girls. They seemed more natural around me and often dropped by to talk over their difficulties. I found that most of the so-called "wild and unruly young radicals" were painfully conventional and lived in mortal dread of differing from each other. Fear tormented them, fear of being unpopular, of not being pledged to a literary society, of failing in their grades, of what other people were saying about them. Most of all they were afraid of disgracing their families by flunking out of college. Some, like Penny who first shocked me by her callous sentiments, spoke of their aversion to their mothers. "She had no time for me" or "She never wanted me" were the reasons most often given. Frequently the thought struck me as I listened that even then Barbara might be pouring out her heart to some teacher or headmistress about her dislike of her mother who had no time for her—only other people's daughters.

She was seldom far from my mind. Something she said that day at the Metropolitan Museum while we were looking at a Corot landscape gave me an idea for Bemis Hall. "It's too bad that we have to stand here with hurting feet, just glancing at these pictures," she commented. "I wish I could take one back to my room at school and live with it for a while." Then all of a sudden another scene flashed through my memory. The year was 1905. One of my classes in French met in the college gallery above the chapel room in Perkins Hall. It was almost unheard of for a student to go there for the sole purpose of looking at the small but excellent collection of paintings. But there was nothing else to do in a course where the teacher was rather dull.

My eyes wandered, unconsciously, to the large canvas facing the class. Something about it gripped my imagination. It was titled, *Pioneers Crossing the Plains*, by Harvey Young. Each time I gazed at it the scene seemed to change. One day a hot, yellow haze veiled the sky, and the next, thunderheads had risen above the far horizon. During the week, tumbleweeds had piled against a clump of sagebrush, the dusty wagon wheels seemed to have sliced deeper into the desert sand; and the faces of the weary travelers turned, longingly, toward the distant, snow-tipped Sangre de Cristos.

Now, many years later, long after I had forgotten the French lessons, I remembered Harvey Young's beautiful picture. And the plan grew for borrowing annually some one of the fine paintings in the college gallery, to hang in Bemis Commons where the girls could "live with them for a little while." *Pioneers Crossing the Plains* was the first to be selected. Leslie J. Skelton, a Canadian-born artist who had come to Colorado Springs for his health, was so impressed that he offered to give six of his beautiful landscapes to the college, as loans each year to the dormitory students in the freshman, sophomore, and junior classes who had made the best scholastic records. And to make the gift complete he added $500 to underwrite the teas at which the pictures were to be awarded.

Meanwhile, I had begun to keep my part of the bargain with Mr. G. Hilmar Lundbeck and the Swedish Steamship Company. Women's clubs and church societies were always looking for free speakers and as soon as it became known that I had returned from Sweden with a lot of colored slides and an interesting story to tell, requests swamped me. But the most gratifying of all was an invitation to take part in the series of six lectures to be given by the faculty as the college's contribution to the community. My intellectual status had moved up a bit.

At last, it seemed as if I had been admitted to the academic fold!

My first talk was at a meeting of the Student Assembly and it had unexpected results. The prospect filled me with stage fright. Usually the undergraduates were restless, inattentive, and often rude during these required weekly "chapels." Even the governor of the state had recently confessed that it was always an ordeal to speak before a student audience. But I had the advantage of being something of a curiosity; few women had ever addressed the whole student body. To my amazement everybody listened intently, as if loathe to miss a single one of the golden phrases. Or could it possibly have been that they were only waiting for my imminent downfall!

Oddly I had decided to save as a highpoint the memorable afternoon with Prince Eugen. After all, it was not an ordinary event to enjoy the hospitality of a famous artist who also happened to be the brother of the king. I described the stately mansion in glowing words and led my hearers through the terraced gardens, gay with fountains, and statues in bronze and marble, and back to the gallery to view the fine art collection. Then we stopped in front of the large painting by Ernst Josephson of the troll playing his violin beneath a silvery waterfall, enticing a mountain nymph on the leafy bank above to cast herself at his feet. I was enchanted all over again by the old folk tale and completely under the spell of my rapt audience. "Josephson had called his painting N-Ä-C-K-E-N," I went on, spelling it out carefully; "in Swedish it is pronounced 'Neckin'——"

Suddenly shouts of laughter filled the room and drowned out my voice. I was nonplussed, for a moment, wondering what I had said to spark such boisterous hilarity. Then, realizing that I was back home, on a college campus where double meanings were the prime source of jokes, I joined in the laughter along with the others and brought my talk to a grateful finish. Certainly I had learned what not to tell about Swedish art!

In addition to the colored slides loaned by the steamship company, I had secured several collections of unusual photographs which I often showed to the students who came in for tea. A senior girl suggested that I write stories about these interesting places. It gave me an idea, and I started with the Colony Gardens of Stockholm. To my amazement, the *Christian Science Monitor*, known to be a good market for beginners, featured it in a Saturday edition. Emboldened by success, I tried another article, called "The Villa of Carl Milles at Lidingö," which was accepted by *House Beautiful*.[1] But writing was a slow, painstaking process for me and took more time than was available from all my other duties. And just then my outside activities were further curtailed by the arrival of an exciting visitor, Countess Maria Loschi from Italy, whom I had come to know at the Conference of the International Federation of University Women in Norway.

It wasn't every day that a genuine countess occupied the guest room at Bemis Hall, and her vivacious manner and dark, sparkling eyes fascinated the girls. Her charm and fluency in English—to say nothing of her title—inspired many social affairs in town and college. Even the Rotary Club invited her to speak at its luncheon, and she addressed the student body at chapel. Her personality was so magnetic, however, that it often got in the way of what she was saying. When pressed for information about the Mussolini regime, she was evasive and emphasized the fact that beggars had been banished from the streets of Rome, slums were rapidly disappearing, and that all able-bodied men had jobs. It was obvious that the contessa had great faith in the Fascisti and their dictator.

[1] *House Beautiful,* March 1929.

But no matter what her political loyalties may have been, few really cared. She was a captivating visitor from a faraway land who had enlivened the staid old college for a little while and left an aura of glamour over the campus long after she had resumed her journey around the world. It was my first brush with Italian nobility, and it made the routine of being the Dean of Women seem colorless and humdrum. I even began to sense a certain incongruity in my speeches to democratic Americans about the developing socialist system of Sweden. Even so, Mr. Lundbeck seemed satisfied and invited me to return and travel to the little-known provinces of Lapland, in the Arctic Circle, and Skåne, "The Granary of Sweden," bordering the Baltic Sea and the Kattegat, and then on to fishing villages such as Fiskebäckskil, on the west coast. It was a tempting outlook but already I was committed to return as Adviser to Women at the Harvard Summer School.

Quite unexpectedly, fate again intervened to alter the course of my career. One day in April a letter came from President Ada Comstock of Radcliffe College, offering me the recently created position as Assistant Dean in charge of residence. For a few minutes I was so overwhelmed with joy that the words danced before my eyes. It had long been my dream to join the small staff at Radcliffe, and at last it was about to be realized! I skipped around my living room like a young girl, waving the half-read letter in my hand. Now Barbara and I would be close together again—her school in Connecticut was only an hour's ride away by train. She could spend her vacations with me and occasional weekends. I might even find a home for us somewhere near the college, and in another year or two she would be a freshman at Radcliffe——

I sat down, breathless, by the big window that looked out upon Pike's Peak and read on: "You would have a suite of rooms in Briggs Hall, the largest of the women's dormitories, and combine the duties of hall mistress with those of Assistant Dean. Your other responsibilities would be largely of a social nature, such as arranging hospitality for distinguished visitors, chaperoning student affairs, presiding over meals, and exercising general supervision over student residential life; and co-operating with student government——"

My heart plummeted; tears welled in my eyes. The very thought of starting over again in another student dormitory sickened me. To what purpose was all the striving and hard work, the time and money spent in study, the travels, if it only meant moving on from one dormitory to another and being forever separated from my daughter? No: I would not do it, I said between sobs, better to stay where I was at Colorado College among friends and associates who respected me! It did not matter if the salary were twice—or three times more than I was getting. I was tired of living an artificial existence, with no freedom, no privacy, no chance for normal social mingling with men. Buried alive among women—women—women——!

Again it was Jessie whose knock aroused me from the wallow of self-pity. "I was just coming down the stairs," she said, "and I thought I heard you call me. Oh Miss Barbee, did you get some bad news——?"

I hastily wiped my eyes and blew my nose. "No, not really. Just a disappointment. I'll get over it—don't worry."

Jessie's sudden appearance seemed to bring me to my senses. I remembered how I had rebelled once against being a Dean of Women and having to live in Bemis Hall. And how, when I had accepted the situation, I had found more gains than losses. I began to think of the advantages of living near Boston, the wonderful music, the theater for Barbara, the sea not far away, and the college one of the most distinguished in the country. Dean Bernice Brown had become one of my good friends, and the weeks at the Harvard Summer School had given me the chance to know President Ada Comstock. Dr. Ruth Merrill, the other Assistant Dean, had once held that position under me at Colorado College. Surely I would not feel like a stranger. And possibly I would not have to live long in Briggs Hall. Miss Comstock might see that I could function just as well in a separate house of my own. She was a reasonable, practical sort of person. It was not hopeless—we could work out a plan together. Barbara could still come for holidays and weekends and stay in the guest room. Something Dr. Ebaugh once said came back to me all of a sudden, "Take one step at a time, and go on from there." And somehow I knew what my decision would be. I would see President Mierow the next day and hand in my resignation.

He had formerly been a member of the faculty as professor of Greek and Latin and was made acting president after Dr. Duniway left, several years before. He was a mild, sweet-natured person who seemed better fitted for almost any calling than that of chief administrator in a strife-torn, small coeducational college. He had been so surrounded by sniping enemies that the Board of Trustees had never mustered enough courage, until recently, to make him president. I had grown very fond of him and especially enjoyed his surprising sense of humor. He always returned from one of his own speech-making trips with a fund of amusing stories, knowing that they would be appreciated by me.

I almost changed my mind when I started to tell him of the Radcliffe offer and my decision to accept it. But I had already written Miss Comstock; there was no turning back. He asked me to keep it quiet for a few weeks in order to give him time to find my successor and to protect him against the pressures that would be brought to bear in favor of many unqualified candidates. One morning, not long before the end of the semester, I received an unforgettable letter from him. It read:

Dear Dean Lee:

It gives me great pleasure to be able to inform you that at the regular meeting of the Board of Trustees of Colorado College, I was authorized to confer upon you, on Commencement Day, the honorary degree of Doctor of Letters.

This matter is to be regarded as confidential.

With best wishes, I am

Sincerely yours,
Charles C. Mierow
PRESIDENT

What a heavy secret to bear in silence! My impulse was to tell it to the students, and all my other friends, and to Barbara. I longed to ring the chapel bell and sing it from the top of Cutler Tower! It was fantastic that I, who had always hoped to be a writer and never succeeded, should one day receive the honorary degree of Doctor of Literature from my alma mater! The temptation to reveal the glorious news was so great that I decided to drive into the mountains and mull it over alone for a long while, before I betrayed the confidence.

Ever since I was a child in Cripple Creek I had always turned to the mountains for stability and quiet, in times of joy or sorrow. Often I went to the lone spruce tree up on Mineral Hill, or maybe to Spring Creek where the water cress grew, or, if it happened to be deep solitude I sought, it might be found as far away as Box Canyon over toward Four Mile Creek. The wild country and I seemed meant for each other, and now, on this day of happiness, "Ophelia Bumps," a bit rackety after seven years, took me to North Cheyenne Canyon and a certain turn-off that ended in a blind road. From there I followed a narrow trail overhung with young aspens and thimbleberry bushes, until it reached the top of a steep mountain and a view of the plains that always took my breath away. Down below, the faint rush of Seven Falls could be heard, swollen by spring rains, and toward the south, the dragon horns of Cheyenne Mountain pierced the glistening sky.

I stretched my arms to heaven and lay in the fragrant shade of a yellow pine and watched a jay preening its blue wings. Here were the only roots I had ever known. One day soon I would trade them for a mortar board with a gilt tassel and the velvet-banded robe of a doctorate. But I would never forget that whatever my strength had been, it was nourished by these mountains.

Commencement came on a shimmering mid-morning in June. The chapel was crowded with townspeople, parents, and students. Their faces were familiar; I had come to know most of them as friends. I scanned the audience as if by some miracle I might see my daughter with her red hair and freckles, but she was still in school 2000 miles away. And then, unexpectedly, I discovered the smiling eyes of Griff Lewis, the Cripple Creek druggist who had helped make possible my graduation from college. He was sitting well up in front just behind the seniors and must have come early to find such a favored spot.

The sight of him after so many years brought flooding memories until he seemed to be the only reality left for me in that large gathering. My mind raced back to the afternoon when, as a timid, young high school teacher with her first warrant in hand, I had gone to his pharmacy to start repaying the loan that enabled me to get my degree. I could see him again reaching for the fishbowl on the shelf, marked "For John's Girl," and he was saying that the money I had thought of as a loan was the gift of my father's friends, "miners, gamblers, businessmen, bartenders, and even old blind Tom, the prospector—they did it in your Dad's memory." His words were so clear that I failed at first to hear President Mierow calling my name. My ears had been deaf to the Commencement address and the hymn, "Oh

Lord, Our God in Ages Past." I was aware only of Dean Hershey adjusting the academic hood with its white velvet border, and black and gold lining, over my shoulders. I caught snatches of a citation being read by the president, which appeared to have no connection with me—"writer and lecturer endowed with a rare gift of expression,"—"interpreter to American womanhood of the ideals and aims of their sisters across the seas,"—"now leaving the campus she knows and loves so well"—"a larger task at Radcliffe College,"—"in recognition of past achievement"—"in anticipation of still greater things to come."

Outside on the lawn, students and friends in bright summer clothes were laughing and chatting, bidding good-bys. Some of them were waiting for me with congratulations and best wishes. But I could not shake off the sense of unreality that had possessed me from the moment I saw Griff Lewis. And now, all at once, he was coming toward me with his hands outstretched and a pleased grin on his face. "Well, I guess you found a way after all," he said jovially, "to repay that debt to your Dad's friends!" My voice choked and I leaned over and kissed him on the cheek. Then, somehow, I made my way across the campus, along the gravel path, down the slope to Bemis Hall.

PART II

THE CHASTENING

XII

The Radcliffe campus, unlike its sprawling neighbor, was a small, homelike retreat not far from the busy center of Cambridge known as Harvard Square. Occasionally, during the summer, I had strolled along its elm-shaded paths on hot days and sat for a while on one of the inviting benches. Although no students were around, a feeling of friendliness pervaded the dignified buildings. I liked to think, as I looked at the windows of Agassiz Hall with their soft draperies and flower boxes, that soon I, too, would have an office there and go in and out as if I belonged. It never occurred to me that my entrance might be the long way around, through the back door.

The four student dormitories bordered a wide expanse of lawn some distance from the campus and were joined together in pairs by common kitchens. Because of my long-standing aversion to living in dormitories, or possibly due to foreboding, I had never ventured that far during my two terms at the Harvard Summer School. But at last the dreadful moment had to be faced. I was expected to report for duty at Briggs Hall ten days before the opening of college. Barbara and I had been staying for a few weeks in the apartment of a vacationing friend, and the school in Connecticut would not open for still another ten days. Unwittingly, I had run head-on into the problem that would finally prove to be my undoing. There was no room for my own daughter in Briggs Hall. In fact, there was scarcely room enough for me in the cramped quarters reserved for the hall mistress. And I found a boardinghouse for Barbara, called the Bide-a-Wee, not far away.

The hall had been closed during the long holidays and a musty odor filled the air. A thick coating of dust covered the floors and the few pieces of furniture that had not been stored. As I glanced at the bare walls and murky windows, Bemis Hall, once the object of my despair, loomed out of the past as a sort of paradise. Oh, for the sight of Jessie and the sound of her familiar voice! Instead of pink and lavender asters on the desk, there was only a typed list of instructions signed by the manager of dormitories. Nine cleaning women would have to be employed at once, it said, "Call the agencies named below." Floors must be waxed; rugs ordered from storage; windows must be washed before the draperies, "locked in the big closet on the second floor," are hung; a schedule of work hours for the help must be arranged——

I floundered in chaos and had no idea where to begin nor how to assemble nine charwomen who would have to double, later, as chamber waitresses. The other hall mistresses, more experienced than I, were swamped with their own problems. It was everybody for herself and woe unto the hindmost! Many other New England colleges were getting ready for the fall semester and housemothers were besieging the employment agencies for help. Nobody who could wield a broom, it seemed, looked twice at the Radcliffe jobs. It was claimed that the hours were too long and the pay below standard. I appealed to the treasurer for more money but he also was a recent appointment and said that he could not make such drastic changes in policy before going carefully into the situation.

Finally the crew was collected and nine pairs of eyes were fixed on me waiting for orders. After a hurried appraisal, I picked a wiry, hard-working individual named Maggie, made her "head maid," and decided to pay her a few cents more out of my own pocket, if necessary. But the tightfisted treasurer relented and advised me to take the extra money from petty cash, temporarily. Maggie turned out to be a veritable major general. In a few hours, closets were unlocked, brooms and dusters began swinging, blankets and rugs had arrived, and drapes were hung in the reception rooms. I had changed my dress for an old smock and soon my nostrils were as black and my face as smudged as the rest of them. They were a fine lot, those cleaning women. Everyone, armed with tools of the trade, fell to and did her utmost. What a different story it was when the students began to pour in on Sunday morning, loaded down with parcels, trunks, and suitcases, and bursting with questions. Two of my stanchest charwomen whom I had appointed as chamber waitresses never showed up nor even gave notice.

I, too, would have escaped from that nightmare of confusion if I had known where to go. Briggs Hall bulged with people— mothers, delivery boys, truck drivers lugging boxes; and girls, girls, girls screaming joyous greetings to each other all over the place. I was bombarded with queries. Has anyone seen a large, square carton marked Lingenfelter, from San Francisco? Little brothers, big brothers, and sweethearts; and still the mothers came! Why does every college girl have to have a mother? There isn't a bookcase in Mary's room—can the janitor put a shelf over the radiator? Why hasn't the steamer trunk been brought up from the basement for number thirteen? Have you change for a quarter, please—I need fifteen cents to tip the messenger boy? No light bulbs are in room ten. Long distance calling Polly Burton, a freshman, she hasn't arrived yet—*where* can Polly be? Can Jan spend the night with her aunt whose husband is a Harvard professor? Why was Iris assigned to Bertram Hall when she expected to be in Briggs? Someone calls me to the telephone.

It is the Dean's secretary wanting to know how things are going and reminding me that I am expected to assist at the reception for parents at four o'clock in Whitman Hall. It is now three-thirty and Maggie has just brought word that the toilet bowl in the north bathroom on the second floor is out of order. Where does one get hold of the plumber——?

I arrived, finally, at the reception, slightly disheveled and out of breath, but, although I was a bit baggy under the eyes, my habit of smiling and shaking hands at such affairs soon took me in charge. Meet Mr. and Mrs. Lampropolis; and Mrs. Lupiansky; and Miss Von Goerkingk—what was *she* doing here!—and Mrs. Podnetsky; and Mr. and Mrs. Epremian. Eyes shining with pride; speech of many accents. Oh, land of dreams come true! America, I salute thee! Then my mind wanders from the scene. I am thinking of the dinner, the first meal to be served at six-thirty in Briggs Hall. Meanwhile, I must decide on a blessing. "The eyes of all wait upon Thee, oh Lord——" How does it go —the one I had said at Bemis Hall for seven years? For the life of me, I couldn't remember. I was wondering if the new chamber waitress would turn up on time, or at all. "We shall keep a few moments of silence, like the Quakers," I said to myself, offering Mrs. Sapinsky another cup of tea, "every girl can speak to God—or not speak—in her own way!"

Things calmed down a bit on Monday, or, rather, the parents had left and the focus of excitement had shifted to the administration building where registration was taking place. My domestic problems, however, took a turn for the worse. Two more maids deserted and for a few days I never knew whether I would be sitting at the head of the dinner table or carrying a tray and napkin. Maggie said that others were threatening to quit. I would have to do something about shortening the hours of work.

I had never been good at figures and barely slipped through freshman mathematics in college. Now I was going to have to work out a complicated schedule that involved rotating hours, days and weeks of service for nine itinerant chamber waitresses. It was a project that almost finished my career as a hall mistress. But some astonishing facts were revealed. I knew nothing about the state laws governing minimum hours of labor but it was certain that we were violating them. The maid on bells, for instance, was on duty nine and a quarter hours every day, except one, until the ninth when the shift increased to ten. The other maids put in eight hours, with thirteen every ninth day. Again I appealed to the treasurer with a plan for improving the service, as well as the morale of the help. He agreed to the employment of a relief maid two and a half hours in the afternoons, which enabled us to stay within the legal limit. It also cut down the turnover.

Before long, I could boast of a happy household and my life became less hectic and frustrating, except for sudden emergencies and such vexing duties as keeping track of guest meals, running a petty-cash account—and coming out even—and collecting for long-distance calls made by forgetful students.

The Massachusetts labor laws did not apply to Assistant Deans, however, and my days and nights were endless and confining. I looked forward as eagerly as any chamber waitress to the one weekend a month allowed me. So far as I was concerned, the important title of Assistant Dean had no relation to me. I suffered most from a lack of privacy. My small, two-room apartment faced the main corridor that led to the dining room. Instead of a picture view of Pike's Peak, the narrow windows looked out on a high board fence. Through the open door of the living room, I was in full sight of the desk in the vestibule and often on call by strange visitors and delivery boys.

My tiny bedroom offered the only escape and even this was a sort of mockery. Buzzers and bells dotted the walls, to alert me in the night if a student entered by way of the basement or back doors. All sorts of alarms reached into my quarters when the maid on bells left at ten o'clock. Students often forgot or lost their keys, and I had to let them in. Two telephones stood on my bedside table—one an extension from the desk outside, also to be switched on when the maid left for the night, and the other for general use in case of emergencies. Having been a Dean of Women at Colorado College proved to be poor preparation for the job as a hall mistress at Radcliffe. Without fully realizing it, my salary had been doubled at the cost of demotion.

The saving grace was the students. They had been selected largely on the basis of fine scholarship, without regard for race, creed, or color. And they, in turn, had come to Radcliffe to get an education, not to resist it. One or two had been allowed to bring their pianos and occasionally I was invited to their rooms for an evening of music and conversation. They talked about their professors, all members of the Harvard faculty, with excitement and enthusiasm, and were well informed on politics and current affairs. They argued about literature and significant authors—Henry James, Sinclair Lewis, Robert Frost; and talked of music—Toscanini's triumphal tour of Europe with the New York Philharmonic Symphony Orchestra; Igor Stravinsky's newest "Symphony of Psalms"; of the best plays—*Green Pastures;* *Grand Hotel;* and *Strange Interlude,* which had been banned in Boston. I was kept continuously on my toes, trying to hold my own with them, and barely succeeding. Never before had I known such mature and lively young undergraduates!

But there was an odd inconsistency in their attitude that I could not fathom. While the self-government organization was completely autonomous, the regulations were as rigid, unreasonable, and futile as they were in my early deanship at Colorado College. Apparently I was going to have to fight this battle all over again. However, there were a few bright spots. For instance, girls who expected to stay out after the ten-o'clock closing hour could take one of the keys in the basket on the outer desk, registering the number in her name. The catch was in the sign-out distinctions. Anyone leaving the hall at eight-thirty or later had to return from a walk with her boy friend by nine, nine-thirty if going for a drive, by eleven if he should take her to a movie, twelve if going to the theater; and so on ad infinitum! Chaperons were required when a girl planned to be out later than midnight. What really happened was that most students simplified the matter and merely signed "show" because it gave them greatest leeway. Then they went wherever they pleased. It would have been impossible to check on their whereabouts in that vast city or to reach them in case of emergency. "Calling" or "movie" might mean anything from motoring to the next village to dining at Tony's Tavern. It was all a pernicious system of deception. But, in spite of my arguments against it, I could not persuade the students to do anything to improve the situation. "The rules are not for us," one girl said, "they are for the Deans, our parents, and the hall mistresses."

Contrary to this opinion, the college administration was well aware of the conditions. Since the rules were student-made, there was little it could do but stand by until the time was ripe for a change. But the Dean, a liberal-minded person and also a distinguished graduate of Radcliffe, came up one day with a brilliant plan. It was designed primarily to relieve the congestion in the halls and at the same time release certain qualified students for independent living, as they might in a family. A fine old residence near the campus was rented and tastefully refurbished, and some fifteen top scholars and leaders were chosen from among the seniors to live there, entirely without adult supervision. Each girl was to be assigned a key and all were expected to observe reasonable hours and to conduct themselves as socially responsible individuals. They moved in just before Thanksgiving and called their new home "Honor House." But

I soon learned that perils existed in the best of self-government systems.

I was so excited by this progressive development that I used it to pour out my rebellion against the evil that had helped make a hypocrite out of me. I wrote an angry article, almost in one sitting, showing up the falsity of the rules that were supposed to control the behavior of women students in colleges up and down the land. The flaming words tumbled from my typewriter and built up to a climactic finish that became the keynote of my own philosophy of education. It was a paragraph, in the form of a parable, taken from a remarkable book called *Creative Experience*,[1] by Mary P. Follett. "Last summer," it read, "I noticed a strange plant in our pasture. I did not know what it was. I had no picture in my mind of what flower or fruit it would bear, but I freed it. That is, I dug around it and opened the soil that the rain might fall on its roots. I cleared out the thistles with which it was entangled so that it might have room to spread; I cut down the undergrowth of small maples near so that it could get the sun. In other words, I freed it."

As I read it over, it occurred to me that at last, perhaps, I had written a piece that might interest Ellery Sedgwick and quickly mailed it off to him before changing my mind. It was called "Censoring the Conduct of College Women."[2] His reply came the day before Christmas, enclosing a check for $100 and making a few minor suggestions. I never knew the far-reaching results that article would have for me, personally, when it was published three months later. It confirmed me in the belief that no constructive thing that one ever does or says is lost, but reappears again in unexpected forms and ways to enrich life.

[1] Harper & Bros., New York, 1924.
[2] *Atlantic Monthly*, April 1930.

The opening of Honor House coincided with the grand ball at the Copley-Plaza, in Boston, which always followed the Harvard-Dartmouth football game. Dartmouth had the reputation of harboring hard drinkers who had little concern for the social amenities. It had never made the grade in social approval on the Dean's list and Radcliffe girls had been forbidden to attend the annual Harvard-Dartmouth dances. But lately there had been much pressure against this discrimination and Dean Brown, possibly flushed with the success of her venture with Honor House, relented. To make doubly sure, she asked me to attend, not as a chaperon but as an unofficial observer. The idea impressed me as being questionable. I recalled that it had taken three plain-clothes men, two deans, and a president to observe the conduct of recent football dances in the little gymnasium at Colorado College. How could I ever check on 800 celebrants in the large ballroom at the Copley-Plaza Hotel!

I managed to persuade the bachelor auditor of my husband's mining company, whose headquarters were in Boston, to accompany me. I had come to know him well on his occasional auditing visits to the Rainbow Mine, in eastern Oregon, where we lived. He was a fine dancer and it turned out to be such a wonderful evening for me that I almost forgot to notice how the young people were behaving. It struck me as being a delightful party in every respect, and, when my feet began to ache, around one o'clock, I decided that my "unofficial" services had been of little value and that I was free to go home. I was midway up the stairs to the cloakroom on the mezzanine floor when a girl coming down stumbled against me. She smelled strongly of liquor. I tried to help her down the steps, but she pushed away from me and mumbled something incoherent. Suddenly I remembered my purpose in being at the Copley-Plaza ball and gave the girl a searching glance but could not recall ever having seen her before. In spite of her rather disheveled golden hair, she was unusually pretty. The suggestion of a dimple in her chin gave the impression of sweet innocence. I felt certain that she was not from Radcliffe—she was not the type. There was comfort in the thought that one case of misconduct out of so many was not a bad record; I could still make a favorable report to the Dean.

But perhaps I should have waited a few weeks, or, again, maybe it was just as well that the Harvard-Dartmouth ball was given a clean bill of health the very next morning.

It was just before the Christmas holidays when Honor House gave its first housewarming reception. The rooms were gay with many flowers and potted plants; the tea table glistened with linen, china, and silver borrowed from the gift supply at Briggs Hall; and the charming young hostesses flitted about in their loveliest dresses. A feeling of pride surged through me that college girls could be, at once, so beautiful and brilliant. As I waited to start through the receiving line, my eye was caught by a vaguely familiar face accented by a dimpled chin and framed by a shock of golden hair. My heart pounded as she held out her hand to me in a warm, cordial greeting. But there was no sign of recognition, and I moved on gratefully, haunted by the ghost of my conscience.

For days and sleepless nights afterward, I wrestled with the dilemma. What should an Assistant Dean and hall mistress do under such circumstances? Was I betraying the Dean's trust by not going to her at once with the truth about the incident at the Harvard-Dartmouth affair. She was a fair-minded college administrator, but I did not know what her attitude would be toward an individual transgressor who was also a member of Honor House. She might be asked to leave in disgrace; her admission to Phi Beta Kappa canceled; she could even be expelled from college. The shattering thought struck me that I would have been the unwilling cause. Suppose it were my own daughter——

Suddenly my course became clear. My responsibility to the student far outweighed my duty to the Dean. I resolved to go out of my way to know the girl better; we might become good friends. And one day when the time was opportune I would talk with her about some of the things that undermine a woman's self-respect and tarnish what the Swedes called her "pride of family." But the confining tasks at Briggs Hall would not let go of me. I never saw her again except at a distance on the day of her graduation, and my memory of her was not as the tippler I met on the stairway at the Copley-Plaza but as the charming young woman who stood in the receiving line that afternoon of the Honor House reception.

XIII

The situation with Barbara had bothered me
ever since moving into Briggs Hall. I had looked forward to
having her spend occasional weekends with me. But there was
no room for an extra bed or even a couch in my apartment and
the one guest room was reserved long in advance for important
visitors. Whenever she came, it was necessary for her to stay
at the Bide-a-Wee, the boarding-rooming house down the street.
At best, it was an unsatisfactory arrangement. She was going
on seventeen and too young to be on her own in a big city
like Cambridge, after the strict supervision of a private school.
I did my best to be with her, but weekends were often my
busiest. There seemed to be no way of keeping one eye on the
occupants of Briggs Hall and the other on my own daughter.
The excursions to the city were not very exciting for a lively,
attractive girl with a growing interest in boys and parties. At
first, she tried whiling away the hours with me in the dormitory
but that, too, was boring. It left her with no adventures or
romances to talk about when she returned to school. Then she
began to come down with severe colds every time she arrived,
which necessitated my finding a substitute hall mistress so that
I could take care of her. These bouts with colds were real pro-
ductions. Her eyes and nose would water and she would cough
and gasp for breath until I trembled with anxiety and, when

the doctor came, it was difficult for him to determine which needed him more, the mother or the child. And twice, on his advice, I took her to the hospital on the verge of pneumonia. Another time she came down with the measles and, when no place could be found to quarantine her in either Briggs Hall or the Bide-a-Wee, the other Assistant Dean, Miss Ruth Merrill, took care of her in her apartment while I hovered in a state of anxiety, fearful of what might strike her down next!

It was during this period that I became aware of the danger of our continued separations. The friends she made were apt to be older boys and girls whom I did not know and who were doing grownup things, even going to night clubs over in Boston and drinking bootleg cocktails. The simple teas and student concerts to which I sometimes took her seemed tame and unglamorous in comparison. She was contantly asking for permission to go with Harvard men to dances which I considered too sophisticated and accused me of being "stuffy" and "old-fashioned." She developed a bitterness toward colleges, "all colleges," which I suspected included their hall mistresses, and declared that she would never go to one anywhere no matter how much I insisted. I could not confess to her that I often shared these sentiments, especially about the social life. How many times I myself had longed to put on my prettiest evening dress and go dancing to Guy Lombardo's orchestra at the Cocoanut Grove! The trouble was that available men at Radcliffe were scarcer even than at Colorado College.

But not for Barbara. She had youth and style and personality—and the loveliest hair imaginable. Harvard students seemed to have some mysterious way of knowing when she had arrived at the Bide-a-Wee and pursued her with attentions. The situation worried me until I began to dread her coming. It did not look well for a girl to live alone, without chaperonage, in a boardinghouse in Cambridge. Then, one weekend when the season of spring parties was at its height, the son of a Colorado friend, a freshman at the law school, invited her to go to a dinner-dance at one of the better hotels in Boston. I had met him and been well impressed, and, since the guest room at Briggs Hall was miraculously vacant, I sent her word that she could go. She wore a new yellow taffeta silk dress for the occasion, and her cheeks were flushed and her eyes sparkled as she called good night and swished out the door with her handsome escort. She had permission, along with the college girls, to stay out until two o'clock but, instead of giving her a key, I said that I would let her in when she rang the doorbell, which would be switched into my bedroom.

It was her first big party and I was as nervous and jittery as if it had been my own debut. I went to bed and started to read Walter Lippmann's *A Preface to Morals,* but couldn't keep my mind on it. I turned the leaves of a copy of the *Atlantic Monthly.* What a tiresome magazine it had become since Stuart Sherman's death! I decided to get up and turn on the radio. It was Saturday night and the blare of jazz bands rent the air. Oh, for something graceful and soothing, like Tchaikovsky's "Waltz of the Flowers"! The time dragged on; it was only twelve o'clock. I put on a robe and went out to the desk. The key basket was almost empty; the house was as still as death. I would have welcomed the sound of laughter somewhere on the terrace; or the smell of a hastily crushed cigarette; or the sight of a girl in a good-night embrace. If only Barbara had decided to come home early—if only——

I went back to my living room and sat in the dark, from where I could see the students checking off their names and hear their keys as they jingled in the basket. It wouldn't be much longer now. In another half hour they would come. Perhaps Barbara would be among them and would not have to ring the bell. At last the little clock in my bedroom struck two, and groups of girls were signing in. Everybody, it seemed, had been dancing somewhere, and, thank goodness, they were all safely returned and chattering noisily up the stairs to their different floors. All, that is, except Barbara. Two-thirty passed, and three o'clock. The only sound I heard was the rapid beating of my heart. Could she have been in a motor accident? I'd better call the police. No; that wouldn't do, coming from a hall mistress at Radcliffe. Reporters were too alert. Telephone the hospitals instead; and I hastily glanced through the maze of them listed in the desk directory, not knowing where to begin. Three-thirty; a quarter to four. The Westminster chimes floated through the night from faraway Harvard Yard. All of a sudden, the bell tinkled faintly and I hurried to the vestibule, unmindful of everything save that Barbara had come home!

She almost fell into my arms as I opened the door. I looked around hastily for the young man but he had slipped away in the dark without saying a word. She was pale and ill and the smell of liquor was on her breath. Somehow I got her into bed and tried to question her, but she could not answer. She was very sick. I could not think of which way to turn and was afraid to call the college nurse, fearful of her report to the Dean. It would be hard to explain that she was not used to any kind of liquor, much less the bootleg poison that Prohibition had produced. I sat on the edge of the bed for a long time, distraught, wondering what to do, blaming myself, cursing my friend's irresponsible son, until at last she sank into deep sleep. Then I snapped off the light and tiptoed down the hall to my apartment.

There was no sleep for me. My mind seethed with rebellion against my way of living. I had reached the end of the long road of compromises, of sacrificing Barbara's good for the sake of a job. From now on, she would come first, no matter what happened to me. I determined to see the president in the morning and explain the circumstances. I would ask her, as I had once asked the president of Colorado College, to let me rent a house off-campus the coming year so that I could make a home for my daughter. There was no need of living in a dormitory, I would say; my experience had been varied and broad enough to enable me to fulfill the duties to greater advantage if my own life could be more normal and Barbara and I could be together.

She was a reasonable woman, easy to talk with and not in any manner forbidding. But I was reminded again that the wheels of college administration grind slowly and that a plan is usually a long time in developing. Once it comes to fruition, it would be easier to uproot the institution than to change what has miraculously become a fixed tradition. The president showed understanding of the serious problem that faced me. She wondered if I had not fully realized the nature of the position when I decided to accept it. I admitted that I knew exactly what the duties were but had hoped that, after a year or two of familiarizing myself with the situation, it could be arranged for me to have a home of my own within easy reach of the halls. I went on to say that my coming to Radcliffe had been the realization of a cherished dream and that I had hoped to stay on for the rest of my career, but my personal dilemma, the obligation to my daughter, made it unwise for me to continue living in Briggs Hall after this year.

The president's eyes were thoughtful as she gazed for a moment through the window at her garden. She was sorry that events had turned out so unhappily for me, she said, and trusted that I would not make any hasty decisions. Her words took on a firmness that I hadn't noticed before. She regretted that the new position had been created by the Board of Trustees for the very purpose to which I objected, that is, providing for an Assistant Dean to live in one of the halls, preferably Briggs.

Both she and Dean Brown, she said, were pleased with the fine start I had made in winning the enthusiastic co-operation of the students. I seemed admirably fitted for the purpose, she went on, and she hoped that after careful consideration I would be able to find a satisfactory solution to the difficulty without feeling the necessity of resigning.

It had been a dignified, well-mannered interview which accomplished little except to clear the air and increase my admiration for the president. Even though she had never married nor borne any children, she had imagination and was genuinely concerned about my problem. But it was beyond her power to change what had been predetermined for the good of the college. I agreed to think it over, but my decision had already been made. A few days later I submitted my resignation.

Aside from the several weeks of grace that lay ahead, and another term at the Harvard Summer School, nothing brightened the future. I seemed to be right back where I started from, but with a difference. A Great Depression gripped the nation. Unemployment was spreading like a plague and men were selling apples on street corners in order to exist. Instead of prosperity such as prevailed in the twenties, banks were closing, business was going into bankruptcy, and curtailment became the theme of employers everywhere. It was a chaotic world for a woman who had so little to offer for a livelihood; and the prospect of what lay ahead was frightening.

Fortunately, the restrictions of Briggs Hall forced me to save a considerable part of my salary, and I figured that by careful planning there would be enough to enable me to rent a small apartment in Cambridge during the winter. A friend, hearing of my predicament, offered to pay Barbara's board and tuition for the senior year at school; and beyond that lay the wasteland of uncertainty. Meanwhile, my article had appeared in the *Atlantic Monthly* and was creating quite a sensation in the neighborhood of Radcliffe and Harvard. Soon letters of enthusiastic approval began to arrive from undergraduates in widely scattered parts of the country. Invitations to speak—at my own expense—came from as far away as Stanford University; and Walter Lippmann quoted an excerpt on the editorial page of the New York *World*. Only the Deans of Women wrote in fear and alarm, warning me that such ill-considered sentiments could undermine the very foundations of women's self-government in colleges. Editor Sedgwick, however, was so pleased with the response that he suggested that I try another paper about the plight of the educated woman who is forced into a career because of her failure to marry.

It was a heady experience to taste the delights of being a real author. I was encouraged to believe that, by devoting my full time to writing, the kind of life I had wanted for myself and Barbara would become a reality. It was the sort of thing I enjoyed most, and I still carted around a box of notebooks filled with impressions and ideas. Stored away in a special place were the beginnings of a book about Cripple Creek, where I had gone with my father and mother during the gold rush in 1892. I wanted to put down my recollections of a girlhood spent in that wild and rugged mining camp. Now perhaps the time was at hand! In spite of the devastation around, I had a means of surviving. I would be freed forever from the suffocating environment of a college. Never again would the fusty smell of old dormitories choke me. From now on, I would be an independent human being, determining my own destiny.

What fine goals and beautiful words! The insidious Depression had crept into every phase of life and by the time I had moved to an apartment in Cambridge, unpacked my books, supplied myself with a typewriter and any number of sharpened pencils and scratch pads, editors were retrenching. The public was not interested in what a former hall mistress had to say about the state of education, or to read her memoirs about a forgotten camp in Colorado. And who cared a whistle about the newest developments in housing in Sweden when people in the United States were losing the roofs over their heads? I wrote feverishly and sold a few things to magazines that promptly folded. The months sped by, leaving me with a sheaf of rejection slips, and I began to inquire at editorial offices for some kind of position in the line of writing to supplement my income.

The article called "The Dilemma of the Educated Woman,"[1] which had been suggested by Ellery Sedgwick, was published but caused few ripples aside from being condensed in the *Review of Reviews*. But I had made several good friends on the *Atlantic* staff who went out of their way to help me make connections with a job. Among them was Teresa Fitzpatrick, the promotion director. She tried to fit me into her department, but I'd had no business training or experience. There was an opening at *House Beautiful*, an Atlantic publication, for a person trained in interior decorating, but that eliminated me.

One day Teresa said, "You know about girls from a great many angles. It strikes me that you would be excellent at conducting a column for parents in a woman's magazine. I'll give you a letter of introduction to Gertrude Lane, editor of the *Woman's Home Companion* in New York. Send her a draft of that proposed story about college admissions and include a copy of your last *Atlantic* article. Come to think of it," she added, "if you can manage to get away, it might be a good idea to go over to New York and present your credentials to Miss Lane in person."

I called her, long distance, at once and made an appointment. She was very different from the tailored, rather mannish seller

[1] *Atlantic Monthly*, November 1930.

of bonds who had dismissed me so abruptly a few years before when I tried to break into the New York investment field. Miss Lane was distinctly an executive type with a charming feminine touch. She was blonde, handsome, and faultlessly dressed. Her large, deep-carpeted office was filled with bookcases and comfortable chairs. A single painting hung above the simulated fireplace, and a huge bowl of early spring flowers stood on her desk. The readers of the *Woman's Home Companion* would have been heartened if they could have seen its editor in her tasteful surroundings, high above the turmoil of a New York thoroughfare. But not if they could have heard the sting in her voice. "There may be something of interest in the admissions piece you have in mind," she said dispassionately, "but first you will have to forget your *Atlantic* style. It wouldn't be appropriate for the kind of magazine we publish." I was so abashed that I forgot the real purpose of the interview and left with as much grace as I could muster. At least she had offered a ray of hope for the admissions article. And that night, back in Cambridge, I wrote in my journal:

> *I am willing to spend my energies extravagantly to achieve success as a writer. I have much in my favor: a background of grim and terrible reality in my childhood; a brief moment of love and happiness in my marriage; and a century, it seems, of widowhood. I shall brew out of it all something good that will bring pleasure and help to others. It is all there for me to draw upon. Even the words which have been so stubborn and shy will come forth gaily, as if to say, "Here we are— clothe us with color, beauty and meaning." Once the dank, academic fog has lifted, I shall be able to sing and fly on literary wings! Oh, to keep the dream and never lose courage!*

Shrinking funds put a strain on flights of fancy. All around me were grim reminders of panic. Apple sellers were multiplying; men and women with gaunt faces walked the streets and loitered in front of employment agencies. Still others were hurling themselves into the Charles River or from the tops of skyscrapers. I doubled my own efforts as the rejection slips accumulated on my desk. In my journal were such notations as, "No luck with Tamblyn-Brown Publicity"; "Application for hostess with Raymond-Whitcomb Travel turned down—tours canceled"; "Interview Personnel Director at Jordan Marsh Store—dropping employees not adding"; "Wrote Ivy Lee, Public Relations, New York—no reply"; "Possibility Boston *Transcript* writing advertising copy—took my name and telephone number——"; "Opening for sorority housemother—no—not yet, not yet——"

So it went. The outlook seemed hopeless. The only bright spot anywhere was the assurance that Barbara was doing well at school. On her last report card the headmistress had written: "Barbara is thoroughly in earnest in her work and is in every way delightful in the family life. She has an excellent mind and with a monthly average of B plus, she should have no trouble succeeding in college. We shall be sorry to lose her when she is graduated."

Then, astonishingly, one morning in April, a letter came from Robert D. Leigh, president of the new experimental college for women which was to be established in Bennington, Vermont. Although I had seen his name in the papers a number of times lately, I had never met him. A mutual friend, Cornelia Stratton Parker, he said, had suggested me for the position as director of admissions for the college. "I have also read your article on 'Censoring the Conduct of College Women,' published several months ago in the *Atlantic Monthly*," the letter went on, "and it seems to me to reveal a very constructive attitude toward the problem of student self-government. It happens to fit closely the ideas we have had regarding the development of our program. Would you be coming to New York in the next week or two? I should like to talk with you about Bennington College."

I was not altogether unfamiliar with the Bennington Plan. For several years, occasional articles had been written about it in the newspapers and magazines, and, as I read, it always struck me as the kind of exciting venture in education in which I should like to take part. I had been particularly impressed by the statement that the plan did not include an official known as a Dean of Women; nor would there be hall mistresses such as those engaged at other institutions to supervise the student residences. Once I had even thought of writing President Leigh about a possible position, but feared that my deanships at Colorado College and Radcliffe would not be a good recommendation. Apparently the *Atlantic* article, which was decidedly unorthodox in its point of view, had helped to wash away my "tradition-encrusted" sins. I found myself on the train, three days later, bound for New York.

PART III

THE AWAKENING

XIV

Bennington College existed, as yet, only on paper and in the dreams of its dedicated friends. Since most of the planning activities were centered in New York City, Mrs. Frederic B. Jennings offered her home at 109 East 73rd Street as headquarters. My appointment was for nine o'clock in the morning and I was more nervous than usual and keenly aware of the bitter lesson I had learned on a similar mission, some eight years before. Whatever happened I resolved not to hurry up the stairs and lose my breath; too much was at stake. Fortunately, an elevator lifted me gently to the second floor where Polly Bullard, the pretty, brown-eyed secretary, was waiting to take me to the president's office.

He greeted me shyly and pulled up a chair at his desk. He must have been in his middle forties but a trace of boyishness in his manner made him seem younger. His blue eyes were set wide apart behind rather thick lenses, giving him a scholarly appearance. I had fortified myself by securing as much information as possible about him before leaving Cambridge. It was not difficult; a number of stories of his appointment had been in the newspapers in recent months. A native of Washington State, he had crossed the country to Maine for his education at Bowdoin College. Upon graduation, Reed College, a young, progressive institution in Portland, Oregon, appointed him to its faculty. Then he journeyed east again for graduate study at Columbia University where he later taught political science. He was professor of government at Williams College when the invitation came to cast his lot with the nebulous Bennington institution, seventeen miles north in Vermont, which had been gestating for almost a decade.

He warmed up as we talked awhile and lost what had impressed me as being a certain diffidence. I, too, relaxed in the consciousness that he liked me. There was nothing pretentious about him. He made no bones of the fact that the Depression had threatened the future of the college. Already the plans had been drastically altered. Instead of a $2,500,000 plant, the amount had been cut in half and wood structures would take the place of the fine, colonial brick buildings the architects had designed. Many corners had been cut for further economies. "But my faith in the idea" he said, "has remained intact, in spite of all the discouraging setbacks and the disastrous state of the nation. Too many devoted, generous people have been working so long toward its fulfillment that it cannot fail. It's an inspiring story."

The clock on his desk pointed to noon. It was hard to believe that three hours had passed since the interview began. I apologized for having used up so much of his busy morning and got up to go. "Wait a minute," he said, "why don't we have lunch together? I know of a small place down on Madison Avenue where the food is excellent. If you would be interested, I'll tell you more about the early struggles of the college." I assured him that I couldn't think of anything more fascinating and he asked Polly to tell Mrs. Leigh, if she called, that he would be back in a couple of hours.

Apparently he was not unknown in the rather intimate restaurant. The headwaiter greeted him with deference and took us to a quiet table where we could talk without interruption.

After giving our orders he sat back comfortably and gave me a shy smile. "I guess I'd better go back to the very beginning," he said as the waiter poured another cup of coffee, "when Dr. Vincent Ravi-Booth, pastor of the Old First Congregational Church, first got the idea of building an 'educational center for girls,' in Old Bennington. Many of his aged parishioners were dying off and the community was sadly in need of an infusion of young life. Dr. Ravi-Booth was a man of action as well as a dreamer and immediately enlisted the aid of Mr. James C. Colgate who offered forty-five acres of land on the lower slope of Mount Anthony as a campus——"

"How wonderful—a college on a mountain!"

"But it didn't work out—there wasn't enough room for future development. Meanwhile, Dr. Ravi-Booth traveled the length and breadth of Vermont, talking about his project. He was a highly respected person and, almost before he realized it, had collected $672,000, and many eminent people in New England had volunteered to promote the plan. Then the good pastor began to worry about having so much money to spend on an educational venture for girls, without the least notion as to how to go ahead with it. He was a minister and all he wanted was a lot of young women around to fill up his church on Sundays. After considerable prayer, so he related, he decided to discuss the problem with the Hall Park McCulloughs who had their summer place in North Bennington."

He called the waiter to bring us another pot of coffee and said something to the effect that he hoped he wasn't boring me. I reassured him. In fact, I could hardly wait to hear the rest of Dr. Ravi-Booth's adventures with his infant "educational center."

"He couldn't have chosen better advisers. Mrs. McCullough consented to be chairman of a committee of twenty-one members who really took over the responsibility of organizing the college." He stirred the sugar in his cup thoughtfully for a moment. "I hope you will meet her soon. For seven years she has worked on this project, day and night, subordinating her rest, recreation, social engagements—everything—to the interests of Bennington College. She and her husband engaged the support of many distinguished leaders in education—William Allen Neilson of Smith, Mary E. Woolley of Mount Holyoke, President Moody of Middlebury College, Ada Comstock of Radcliffe——"

I perked my ears at hearing this familiar name. "Miss Comstock, too, lent her support——?"

"She contributed much in the way of down-to-earth common sense—you must know her well."

"Not as well as I should have liked," I said simply.

Then he looked at me searchingly and said, "What was the real reason for your resignation from Radcliffe? I am pretty well informed about most of your training and experience, but I still can't fathom why you gave up such an opportunity at one of the greatest women's colleges in the country. Maybe I don't know all the facts."

I told him that it was entirely a personal problem. I felt that it was more important to make a home for my daughter than it was to live separated from her in a dormitory for the rest of my working life. "I couldn't face it," I said, "and decided to put a quick end to it." Then, in fear and trembling, I asked him a question. "Do you plan to employ hall mistresses in the student residences when Bennington is built?"

He threw back his head and laughed. "Never! You can forget that prospect! There will be faculty apartments for couples in each of the twelve residences, who will live there as friends, not supervisors of conduct. We expect the girls to set up their own standards and rules and to live by them." He pushed back his chair a bit and eyed me with a knowing smile. "Furthermore," he went on, "there will be no Dean of Women, nor even a Dean of the college. You see, Bennington College will be quite atypical." He reached in his pocket and brought out a pamphlet. "You will be interested in reading this when you have time," he said, handing it to me. "It is a brief description of the main features of the Bennington Plan. Dr. William H. Kilpatrick of Teachers' College wrote most of it. You probably know of him. He's at present chairman of our Board of Trustees."

Indeed I had heard of Dr. Kilpatrick; he was no stranger to anyone who worked in the field of education. I put the brochure in my handbag and said that I would read it that night at the hotel. The president went on with the story, telling more of the early struggles and naming many of the supporters who later became members of the Board. The list sounded as if it had been taken from Who's Who Among American Women. Among others they included Mrs. Joseph S. Swan, Mrs. George S. Franklin, Mrs. Irving Warner, Mrs. Ernest Poole, Mrs. Clarence M. Woolley, Mrs. Dwight Morrow, Miss Frances Perkins, Mrs. Dorothy Canfield Fisher, Mrs. Frederic B. Jennings—

"It was Mrs. Jennings who, after the Colgate offer was withdrawn, gave us 140 acres on a sunny slope of her farmland in North Bennington," and then he added, "we couldn't have wished for a more beautiful location!"

Just then a waiter came to the table, saying that someone wanted him on the telephone. The president hastily glanced at his wrist watch. "Good gracious!" he exclaimed. "It's five o'clock, and that's doubtless my wife reminding me that we have a dinner engagement—she has probably called every one of my haunts in New York trying to find me!" It was the rush hour outside, with crowds hurrying in all directions. He shook my hand hastily and said, "I can't assure you a thing just now.

This Depression has played havoc with our fund raising. So many pledges have had to be canceled. The whole idea may have to be given just—but I haven't lost hope yet. I'll get in touch with you as soon as there is anything definite."

It had been a long day but I was not too weary to read the Bennington Plan before going to bed. Every word struck a responsive note in me—the individually arranged programs of study, inclusion of the arts with the usual academic subjects, the small, home-like student residences, and the Winter Field and Reading Period. I thought I had finished with all colleges, but here was something different. It seemed as if it were the goal toward which I had been groping blindly ever since my days at Colorado College. "The college was conceived," the preamble stated, "as a result of dissatisfaction with existing women's colleges and a desire to carry out a consistent educational program derived in part from the work of the progressive schools, in part from successful innovations already tried out in other colleges, and in part from educational theories which leading educators had long wanted to put into effect."

I mulled over the exciting program far into the night, and with every sentence my longing to take part in it increased. What a wonderful venture it would be to help create such an institution! Here was a college starting from the ground up, free from the conservatism of established habit, of tradition dear to alumni, taking what is good of the old, adapting it to the better understanding of present problems. It would be the kind of college where student responsibility would be stressed and scholarship would not become a cause of embarrassment or apology. The life of the mind and love of learning would be of first importance.

The president had said that he had thought of me in connection with admissions, and I read and re-read the long statement of aims. "No college entrance examination will be required; neither Latin nor any other particular school course will be necessary." It went on to say, "A girl who may have what is called "a blind spot" in a subject such as mathematics or a language will be considered for admission provided she is outstanding in her other studies. A student who shows promise and genuine interest in learning will be admitted on the basis of her total record, plus the recommendation of her teachers, the principal and a personal interview with an expert admissions director."

This last requirement gave me pause, but at that hour, with the lights still blinking in the skyscrapers and traffic humming in the street below, I felt equal to any assignment. I would study the best thought of other educators, in books and magazine articles. I had never known of a "director of admissions"; such officials had not yet been invented out west and I had heard of only two or three in eastern colleges. I would talk with them and acquaint myself with some of their problems and experiences. The "love of learning" would begin with me!

But it was the next paragraph that caught my eye. "We propose to emphasize personnel work," it read, "starting with the student's admission and going through her whole undergraduate career. With the guidance of a Mental Hygienist, the College will take account of her emotional as well as intellectual growth and will establish a program of counseling to ensure that she has learned in her own way, at her own pace, and according to her own capacities and developing purposes. Such is our program," it concluded; "it is a general rather than a detailed plan. This would trouble us more if we did not know the danger lurking in perfection of detail made too far in advance of actual experience."

I could think of little else during the five-hour train trip back to Boston. It seemed to me that I would never be able to contain myself until hearing again from President Leigh. But the days and weeks dragged by without any further news. I tried to forget my anxiety by writing feverishly. The *Woman's Home Companion* accepted a brief article called "When a Girl Goes to College." One or two short reports appeared on the education page of the New York *Times.* But writing such pieces was a losing game for me. I began to think more and more of the book I'd had in mind so long, about my childhood years spent in Cripple Creek, and I filled my journal with notes. Someday, perhaps, something might come of it. But not yet—my money would be gone in little more than two months and jobs were scarcer than ever. And there was Barbara to think of, facing the desperate world armed only with an embossed diploma from a private secondary school.

Still no message from President Leigh. It was nearing the end of May and I was about to conclude that the appointment had gone to someone else, or that the Bennington Plan had finally faded into the dream from which it sprang because of the Depression. Then, at last, the telegram came inviting me to attend a meeting of the Executive Committee of the Board of Trustees at the New York home of Mr. and Mrs. Hall Park McCullough. "You are being considered for the post of Director of Admissions," the message read, "and it is well for you to be prepared to answer questions and talk rather informally on the Bennington admissions procedure."

My hand trembled so that I could hardly read, partly from joy, but mostly from fright. The very idea of having to face a quiz on the subject of college admissions by a group of such renowned educators as William Heard Kilpatrick threw me into a state of nervous strain. I was conscious of being the first member of the staff to be interviewed by the trustee committee. The president's later procedure followed a more formal but less formidable practice of presenting nominations orally, with supporting evidence, at trustee meetings. But there was no cushion for me, no softening of the sharp point of contact. Fate seemed to hang in the balance!

My worries turned out to be unnecessary. The friendliness of the small group immediately disarmed me. With the exception of Dr. Leigh, they were all strangers to me—Mrs. McCullough with her gracious, unassuming manner; Mrs. Swan making a point in her quick, concise way of speaking; Mrs. Woolley with her penetrating comments, often touched with humor; Professor John Coss of Columbia University plying his searching questions. The president was obviously trying nobly to be unbiased but now and then he added a word of praise as if to stiffen my backbone.

The most unforgettable of all was Dr. Kilpatrick. He sat over by a window in a deep chair that almost swallowed up his slight figure. His silky, snow-white hair, parted in the middle, seemed to accent the youthfulness of his face. I was inclined to view him with awe but his quiet, modest way of speaking soon disarmed me. He framed his questions slowly, deftly, as if he himself were still seeking answers. To my astonishment, latent ideas of which I had been unaware until then began to emerge and take shape. Books on educational philosophy by John Dewey, over which I had pored during the long weeks of waiting, suddenly came alive with meaning. Even the lectures at the New School for Social Research grew vivid in memory and gave me confidence. It seemed as if all the rich and vital things I had ever learned from Dr. Ebaugh and Stuart Sherman, and Annastina in faraway Sweden, and the many other enlightening friends I had known through the stormy years, were mustered now to stand by me in this critical hour. I could not recall, the next day, just what I had said, but when Mrs. Leigh rescued me from the business meeting that was to follow, I had the warm, beautiful feeling that all was well.

XV

President Leigh thought it important for me to begin my duties in Bennington on the first of July. It was with a feeling of release that I sent in my resignation as Adviser to Women at the Harvard Summer School. I hoped it would be the last time I would ever have to live in a college dormitory. Several farm buildings and a white cottage called Cricket Hill stood on the Jennings land which had now become the campus. The chicken coop had already been made over into temporary administrative offices, and Dr. Leigh said that I could probably arrange to live at the near-by home of the Loomises, "pioneer Vermonters," who could also make room for Barbara.

She would be graduating from school in another ten days and I could hardly wait to tell her all the good news. But she was not impressed with the idea of spending a lonely summer in Bennington while I was busy in an office all day. In fact, she had her own plans. She wanted to go to the Phidelah Rice School of Dramatics in Martha's Vineyard; and in the fall she would like to attend the Neighborhood Playhouse in New York. She had just passed her eighteenth birthday and had a mind of her own, and I, who had become imbued with the Bennington philosophy, could not consistently deny her the chance to pursue her own "vital interests." The prospect of another long separation filled me with dread. In the past year or two I was conscious of her gradually growing away from me— a sort of withdrawal within herself that I could not seem to stem. It was as if we had become strangers unable to communicate with each other. But at last the longed-for day had come and our home was about to materialize! Perhaps I might even persuade her to attend Bennington College when it opened in another year, where she could major in dramatics. The thought gave me a light heart, that first morning, as I hurried along the dirt road from the Loomis farm to my office in the renovated Chicken Coop.

The president was waiting in front of Cricket Hill cottage to take me on a tour of the grounds. We strolled past the big, rusty-red barn, shaped like a U, which was destined to play such an important role in the life of the college. Just then it was being used for storing old equipment. Down the slope a short way rose the slight knoll on which the Commons, the only brick structure, would stand "like a New England Town Hall overlooking the village Green." Altogether there would be twelve student residences built around the Green, each one housing twenty girls. "We shall erect four every year until the program is completed." He described them in such vivid detail that I could almost see the students walking along the paths on their way to the library in the Barn, or going for a mid-morning snack in the community store in the Commons.

We stood for a while gazing out over the beautiful countryside. Dew glistened on the foxtail grass and bluebells; larks sang from the fence posts, and the fragrance of sweet clover filled the air. My eyes followed the road down past the old graveyard to the highway which for a few years would be the main entrance to the campus. Beyond, the languid Walloomsac River threaded its course through a tangle of willows and cottonwoods. Across the narrow valley on a wooded plateau, the stately obelisk of the Bennington Battle Monument rose among colonial mansions against the background of Mount Anthony. Not far to the left, the Old First Congregational Church thrust a slender white spire heavenward, a reminder that the vision of a college for women in that idyllic setting was first conceived in the mind of its pastor, Dr. Vincent Ravi-Booth.

"In these peaceful surroundings," Dr. Leigh said reflectively, "it's hard to believe that in the cities, only a few hours away, men are walking the streets desperately searching for work, and some, in hopeless despair, are destroying themselves. Creating this college is an act of faith in the future, not found today, perhaps, anywhere else in our country."

We walked back slowly to the long, low building that had once housed dozens of chickens and ducks. Only three of us made up the staff—the president, the treasurer, and myself. A few weeks later, Myra H. Jones, the newly appointed comptroller, was due to arrive, and in January we would be joined by Gladys Y. Leslie, the librarian. Together, in our various capacities, we made up the skeleton of the infant college. Naturally I felt that my responsibility offered the greatest challenge. Within the brief space of a year I was going to have to find, somewhere in the panic-stricken nation, a freshman class of eighty girls whose parents didn't mind having them experimented on, and who could somehow scrape up the wherewithal to pay the $1685 tuition fee!

Fortunately the admissions system had been embodied in the Bennington Plan long before I came on the scene. According to the president, it was not entirely original but had grown out of the advice and practices of the more experienced college admissions directors. It was merely part of the "swing of educational tendency." There was nothing for me to do for the next few months, he went on to explain, but to "evaluate and implement the prerequisites" set up by the Education Committee of the Board of Trustees. The casual assignment left me aghast!

Many colleges had begun to adopt various forms, widely copied from each other, which were to be filled out as part of the admissions procedure. As a rule they were devised by amateur psychologists like myself for the purpose of securing information that might reveal the true nature and abilities of the unsuspecting applicant. I boldly appropriated what seemed good, making adaptations that suited the Bennington situation, and here and there adding a master stroke of my own. Finally, after many conferences with the president and with the help of a skilled secretary, a set of three forms was approved, one for the school record and recommendations, another for the parents, and the third for the girl. She was asked to write a two-page essay on her main interests and extracurricular activities, to list the books she had read recently and the music she had enjoyed, to tell of her travels and hobbies, and, lastly, to give her reasons for wanting to attend an experimental college like Bennington. It was quite an order for an eighteen-year-old applicant, but of course it was expected to reveal between the lines the quality of her mind and the important traits of her personality.

I had much to learn from these forms, especially the applicant's, when they came back to roost in the Chicken Coop. For instance, some of the candidates from widely separated places had written identical answers to the question: "What books have you read recently——?" The list invariably included the novels of Hugh Walpole, Galsworthy, Dickens, and Hardy; and the poetry of Keats, Frost, and Sandburg. On making a few inquiries, I found that these books were required collateral reading in most high school courses in English literature. Apparently my candidates had not ventured far from the classroom in their literary foraging. But it was not too serious, I reasoned; such information would still be useful as an approach to the personal interview which was also a feature of the admissions plan.

I set out on my voyage of discovery with a high heart, soon after schools had opened, the middle of September. Barbara had enrolled at the Neighborhood Playhouse and was living at the Rehearsal Club, a moderately priced and sensibly supervised "home away from home" supported by philanthropic New York women for young, aspiring actresses. My able secretary had made out a schedule of appointments with the girls and their parents in towns and cities as far away as Chicago, who had sent in applications and completed the forms. I looked forward to meeting them with considerable trepidation, feeling in some respects like a prospector searching for gold and equipped only with a whimsical divining rod. Although I had lived and worked among college students for a number of years, I was a novice in the art of interviewing. A few books of advice and suggestions had been written, usually by personnel officers in industry, and I had read them with the greatest care. But when I came face to face with my nervous young victim, I was conscious of nothing but her appealing helplessness and forgot the counsel of the experts.

Sometimes she became inarticulate with fear and her eager mother would then jump to the rescue. My next problem was to detour around the parent as tactfully as possible—the books hadn't mentioned this emergency—and work back to the daughter who by now had doubtless seen through me and regained her composure. After these preliminary skirmishes, we usually settled down to an hour of pleasant conversation, with me intent on getting some idea of her "latent ability" and with her trying, artfully, to find out how late the students could stay out at night, and how far was Bennington from Williams College.

In time, either the director of admissions became more adept or the applicants grew wiser, for the interviews usually developed into an exciting experience for all concerned. I was never deceived about their subjective nature, but I began to detect little signs of an individual's growing maturity. I noticed, for instance, her diction, the extent of her vocabulary, and how she used it to express her ideas. I watched for a show of self-confidence and vitality in bearing. Doubtless, my conclusions were often wrong. The intangibles of character were not to be caught so easily in a net. But there was one result on which I had not counted. Applicants were frequently recommended as "the ideal Bennington type," a term which annoyed the president and me, for we had always thought of our students as being custom made! Evidently it had come to mean a girl who spoke cultivated English, and possibly a smattering of French, and who had poise, self-assurance, and personality plus, in addition to marked intellectual and artistic gifts. A rare combination, indeed, which probably frightened away some pedestrian but worth-while candidates. I was unaware of having any particular image in mind but, if there had been one, she would probably have been a cross between a brilliant student, nick-named "Peaches," at Colorado College, and Alison, the girl with the dark brooding eyes of her poet-mother, at Radcliffe.

The question of main or strong special interests always came in for a great deal of discussion. It never failed to quicken the tempo of the interview and usually left me in a state of wonderment. Every other girl, it seemed, wanted to become either an artist, a composer, a writer—notably of poetry—or an actress. Now and then an exception happened along to flabbergast me, such as Elizabeth whose talents lay in carpentry and musical bell ringing—an accomplishment which her parents had brought with them from England. The college offered no instruction in either of those fields and Elizabeth's mind seemed to go blank when she tried to think of other studies which might be pursued. But her school grades were fine, her background excellent, and I was particularly attracted by her intelligent eyes and quiet dignity. I decided to take a chance and admit her, hoping that in our system of "trial majors," and with a faculty counselor, sooner or later she would discover a main interest.

It was the first of many other compromises I was going to have to make under the item called special interests. My faith in their validity had begun to waver. There were girls, for instance, who wanted to major in Chinese philosophy, or the tribal customs of the Navaho Indians—this one had been on a trip through New Mexico the summer before—or the fishes in Boston Harbor. Several declared simply that they "liked children" and wanted to work with them in some way, but Jane, the attractive New York debutante, preferred animals. She was "mad about horses" and planned to be a veterinarian. Did Bennington offer any courses in animal husbandry?

Then there was Lorie! She yearned to do research in a disease of turkeys, called blackhead, which was causing great losses to farmers. So anxious was she to get started that she applied a year in advance for admission to the second entering class. This was something to boast about to the trustees! Her grades were high, especially in science, and her intelligence quotient well above average. Here was Bennington's answer to prayer! I threw discretion to the winds and admitted her on the spot, provided she kept up her record through the senior year.

Suddenly she caught me off-guard with an astonishing request. Could she bring along eight or nine turkeys for experimentation? Something warned me to delay the matter until I could talk with the president. I couldn't recall ever seeing anything but pickled cats in the laboratories at other colleges. But then, Bennington was going to be different, not bound up in a lot of foolish rules and regulations. And Lorie seemed eager to have the thing settled; she even mentioned the frightening possibility of going elsewhere! The more I pondered, the more fascinating the idea became. Lorie, it struck me, was the kind of serious student for whom Bennington College had been founded. So I agreed, tentatively, to the turkey arrangement, with the understanding that it would also have to be approved by President Leigh, and on condition that she would take full responsibility for the care and feeding of her birds. She agreed and a good spirit prevailed all around.

Many of the interviews were held at high schools where I also talked with principals and teachers and further explained the Bennington Plan. Some of them were honestly concerned. It was felt, for instance, that so much freedom in selecting courses might lead to dilettantism. Fears were expressed that too great emphasis on the individual would result in a lack of *esprit de corps*. Mathematics and language instructors seemed greatly disturbed about the college's intention to label these basic subjects as "tool" courses. Schoolmen had heard with dismay that young, unseasoned teachers were going to be engaged, some even without advanced degrees! They earnestly questioned the wisdom of this policy.

Students usually lingered after my assembly talks to ply me with questions. They seemed enchanted by the college that was going to start in a barn, and their queries often put a strain on my resourcefulness. After all, Bennington was still a dream place with no buildings except a few farmhouses, no faculty to point to with pride, no alumnae to give it prestige, and not even one student. While it was a very real institution to me, I couldn't always be certain of the answers. For instance, what about pets? Again and again the matter came up. Could a girl bring her "adorable" dachshund?—or her "darling Persian kitten?" My first impulse, based on sad experience, was to shout an emphatic no. But it occurred to me that anything could happen at this unorthodox college and I hedged, without making any commitments.

Parents, too, waited for further enlightenment. They were especially apprehensive about the reported lack of supervision under which their daughters would live in the dormitories. Freshmen were not experienced enough to be entirely on their own, they asserted, and should not be left alone without housemothers to watch over them. I was happy to be able to allay their fears by describing the faculty suites that would be part of each student residence. The extra cost of the Winter Field and Reading Period also troubled them. They said that they would neither want their daughters idle at home for two months when other girls were in school, nor did they relish the prospect of their traipsing around New York, Boston, or other points east on some kind of fantastic "project," where nobody kept an eye on them; and all this at the family's expense!

This was one of the most difficult features of the college to explain, for, so far, the Winter Field and Reading Period was only a beautiful statement of purpose in the educational plan. As so often happened, there were no past experiences to lean on, no splendid examples to quote; and President Leigh was a thousand miles away, usually, making speeches to other groups. I was never certain that my improvisations would agree with his ideas. However, we had a philosophy in common and a few powerful influences carried me over the hurdles. Oddly enough, one of them was the Depression. I quoted the president's remark about building the college in those dark times as "being an act of faith in the future." And my descriptions of the campus surrounded by orchards and fields of clover, and of the library and classrooms in the Barn, and the administrative offices in the Chicken Coop, seemed to have the nostalgic appeal of the little red schoolhouse and inspire confidence.

It was not surprising to find many parents willing to sacrifice to enable their daughters to share in such a pioneering venture. Sometimes their expectations even exceeded my own and became a source of embarrassment. Disillusioned mothers and fathers would endow the college with a magic power to which it had never laid claim. If only the problem child could go to such a place, all her difficulties would be solved and she would live a happy, successful life ever after! But Bennington had not been organized or staffed as an institution for emotionally disturbed girls and such applicants were usually refused in spite of impassioned pleas from the family, the minister, and intimate friends. The president, when he had the facts, stood by me loyally in such cases, often at the risk of losing some of his own friends. Doubtless we made mistakes on that score.

Even the high cost of tuition, room, and board did not turn out to be the great obstacle I had anticipated. The policy of making reductions for the student whose family could not pay the full amount attracted applicants in varied financial circumstances. The promise of part-time jobs in the library, offices, and dining rooms offered further chances for cutting expenses. It was not unusual for a Boston or New York debutante whose parents had been wealthy until the stock-market crash to be among the first to apply for a place as a waitress. Work, no matter how humble, had come to be regarded by young and old as a privilege in a society stricken with unemployment.

It was spring when I returned to the campus. I had spoken in more than fifty high schools and at many luncheons, club meetings, and before other groups. I was glad to get back to Vermont. Patches of melting snow still lay under the trees in the McCullough woods, and sap dripped into the buckets hanging from the sugar maples. The campus was teeming with activity. Pounding hammers and whining saws filled the air with cacophonous sounds and a sense of urgency. Four student houses, gleaming white and looking like toys, stood primly in the meadow where not so long before wild strawberries and forget-me-nots had flourished. The pink brick walls of the Commons building were reaching skyward. Stalls and haylofts had been ripped from the Barn, and two-by-four ribbings marked off the library, the faculty lounge, and administrative offices. Skeleton partitions were rising on the second floor, and in the left wing reserved for laboratories, lecture hall and classrooms. In spite of all the stretching and straining, however, the old Barn retained its rural shape and character. Cricket Hill cottage, a few yards away, had also come alive. Smoke drifted from the chimney, lights brightened the windows at evening, and the delicious smell of fresh baked rolls floated from the kitchen. The Loomises had taken over and were serving lunches to the office staff, and Gladys Leslie and I had moved temporarily into the two upper bedrooms.

But the most elating sight of all was four miles away from the campus, across the valley on the sunny side of Mount Anthony in Old Bennington. A beautiful white colonial homestead, supported by stately columns and half-hidden in a grove of elms, was being made over into attractive apartments for the librarian, the comptroller, an instructor in the English department who would come later, and the director of admissions. It had been a gift to the college from the family of a trustee and was named Hall House. I had bought a Ford roadster and scarcely an evening passed without driving over to feast my eyes on the heartening scene. Soon I would have the "room of my own" I had always been longing for, and, at last, Barbara was going to have a home and might even change her mind about not wanting to attend the college. But wherever we wandered, it would be a place to come back to, a spot on the face of the earth where we belonged.

XVI

The Chicken Coop had taken on the aspect of a beehive that first summer, with the treasurer scouring the countryside by letter and telegram for more money, while the president conferred with architects, contractors, prospective teachers, and members of the Board of Trustees. And, of course, he kept a weathered eye on the list of admissions. For what good was a college without students? Often the applications seemed to be rivaling the fluctuations of the stock market. At the moment when a full quota appeared to be in sight, several cancellations would ground our soaring spirits. Toward the last of July, however, when the admission fee of ten dollars was no longer refundable, seventy-five applicants had been accepted and enough were held in reserve on a waiting list to assure an entering class. By doubling some of the rooms we were able to accommodate eighty-five girls, with two graduates of the local high school.

It had been a long, uphill pull. The goal never could have been reached without the help of many others, principally the indefatigable members of the Board of Trustees. They not only planned to enroll their own daughters but interested influential friends in following their example. They arranged large monthly luncheon meetings at the Colony and Cosmopolitan Clubs in New York, and the Chilton Club in Boston, where Dr. Kilpatrick, President Leigh, and I usually spoke. My school visits were often supplemented by their personal notes to principals and headmistresses. It struck me in those beginning years that Bennington College became a reality not because of its appealing location on a Vermont farm, nor gifts of money, nor even in the uniqueness of its program but because of the quality and character of the men and women who were on its early committees and the first Board of Trustees.

Our combined efforts continued to bring results. It looked as if an avalanche had been started from the mail that had piled up on my desk. Requests for information ranged from the graduate student who wanted material for her Master's thesis to the parent who wished me to send her a list of private schools which would ensure her daughter's acceptance at Bennington four years hence. It meant walking gingerly to avoid the pitfalls. Applications for the second entering class were already coming in to bring cheer. And the girls, who would be arriving on campus in a few weeks, seemed to be bubbling over with questions. How many party dresses would they need? Could they wear shorts? Should they bring their own blankets? And would someone please send a list of the rules and regulations? But the question about being allowed to have pets was so persistent that it seemed as if it were part of a conspiracy. Sooner or later the matter would have to be settled, so I approached the president about it one day during a lull.

"What do you think about permitting the girls to bring their pets to college?" I asked. "Many of them want to know."

"What do you think?" he said noncommittally.

"I'm not in favor of it."

"Why?"

"Well——" I was about to add, "speaking from experience," but I suddenly remembered that he did not think much of a

Dean's experience. So I simply stated that pets could be a serious nuisance in the student houses.

"In what way?"

"They have to be fed, for one thing, and the food is apt to be slipped from the dining rooms and kitchen. Also," I said, gathering momentum, "animals have habits, and if a girl oversleeps mornings, nature will take its course without respect to floors and rugs. Furthermore," I went on, feeling that he was about convinced, "one dog—or cat—leads to another and the campus is likely to be overrun with animals. Frankly, I think it would be a great mistake to let them get started."

He had listened attentively and was silent for a moment. Then, all at once, his face lit up boyishly. "Why wouldn't it be an excellent venture in practical education," he said, "for the students themselves to reach that conclusion? Give them the responsibility of dealing with the situation if it becomes a problem. I'm for letting the pets come." He gave me a reprimanding glance. "You and I will have to watch ourselves. We may often want to take the reins in our own hands but the temptation should be resisted!"

"Very well," I said, a bit dismayed, "but we can expect all sorts—dogs, cats—perhaps even a flock of turkeys!"

"Good!" he laughed, pleased with the idea. "It'll be fun to see what happens!"

College opened shortly after Labor Day, 1932. The campus was in a dither of activity. Faculty members were pouring over the brief biographies I had written about each student by way of introduction before their conferences. The president had a gift for selecting personable as well as competent young instructors. Their average age that first year was said to be around thirty-two and some of them looked even more youthful than the undergraduates whom they were to teach and guide. A few well-known names were among them: Genevieve Taggard,

the poet; Kurt Schindler, the composer-director who founded
the Schola Cantorum in New York; Irving Fineman, the novelist—and my neighbor in Hall House; and Edwin Avery Park,
the artist whose wife, the former Frances Fenton Bernard, had
eloped with him when she was Dean of Smith College.

Then there was Dr. Wilmoth Osborne, the tall, dominant
college physician. She had not quite completed her psychiatric
training but it was said that she knew so much about the why
of human behavior that the very sight of her caused me to slink
within myself and guard my speech. Ever since my surreptitious
visits with Dr. Ebaugh, ten years before, I had hoped to find
a mental hygienist attached to a college staff. Now at last my
wish had been realized. No longer would anyone be suspected
of being peculiar if she sought the counsel of a psychiatrist.
Everything was going to be out in the open. A girl would feel
as free to consult the doctor about her habit of lying as she
had been to get a prescription for tonsillitis. And she would be
given straight, clean-cut advice. Oh happy day! I never thought
I'd see it come to pass!

I stood for a while on the terrace in front of the Commons,
taking in the colorful scene, trying to convince myself that it
was actually real. The Green looked more like a movie set with
its neat paths and shrubs and two gleaming white residences on
either side. Flowers bloomed in the window boxes, and graceful
elms, transplanted full grown from the Jennings estate, shaded
the gravel road. Friendships, too, had begun to bud. Girls in
shorts lay on the grass sunning themselves together as if they
had known each other always. Some strolled arm in arm, while
their dachshunds or Scotties played hide-and-seek among the
butterfly bushes. My memory had never been one of the best,
but I recalled the name of every member of the class, where she
lived, and her special traits of personality. Most of them were
from Massachusetts, New York, and New Jersey, but there was

a scattering from states as far west as Oregon. They were out of a variety of backgrounds—small towns, large cities, and rural communities. Their fathers were lawyers, or doctors, or musicians, with many businesses represented and trades such as printing and masonry.

If a composite picture of Bennington's first students could have been drawn, it would have been of a girl slightly under eighteen, an Episcopalian, and the daughter of a lawyer. Probably she was a graduate of a private school in or near Boston, and her headmistress would have described her as a leader. While her special interest was likely to be in the field of social studies, with music and English literature close seconds, she hoped someday to write as a hobby. And her recreation would be found in sports, especially swimming and tennis. She expected to marry and have four children.

The Williams men, a few miles south, promised to see that she didn't become a spinster. The president and I had talked blithely, at first, of the advantages in having a men's college so near. It would give Bennington some of the benefits of coeducation without many of the headaches. We were not so sure however, when the boys began to invade the campus on bicycles, in jalopies, and fancy sports cars. It was a new experience for them having eighty-five "dream boats" only twenty minutes run, up the dugway. But not all of them came seeking romance. Some claimed to be merely curious to see what kind of girl would go to such a "cockeyed institution." Others made no bones of resenting the intrusion of women in their hitherto unviolated corner of New England and showed their scorn by getting drunk and creating incidents. One dark night, during a mild epidemic of measles, a group of them terrified the occupants of Dewey House by climbing through a window just to see, so they explained later to their Dean, if they could catch the disease from such "hand-picked dolls."

Indignant Bennington girls immediately went into action. Under the leadership of Elizabeth, the carpenter and bell ringer, who had been elected president of Community Government, resolutions were adopted making it clear to marauding males from over the state line that no future nonsense would be tolerated. President Leigh commended the undergraduates for the way in which they had risen to meet the situation. A few of the older faculty members were not so confident. It was a fine ideal, they said, putting freshmen on their own, but it simply wasn't realistic. "We'd better be prepared for the worst," one instructor warned, "*anything* could happen!" But it wasn't always the students who caused concern. The president's idea of engaging attractive as well as scholarly young teachers had its romantic complications and it must have irked him occasionally to have to act in the capacity of a Dean of Women, and to remind them that they were expected to live up to the standards of Community Government.

Meanwhile, the campus had begun to look like headquarters for Pets Unlimited! Dogs of all colors, shapes, and sizes chased over the lawns and flower beds, barking and fighting. Cats of aristocratic breeds mingled shamelessly with their alley brethren and turned night into a howling brawl. White mice snuggled contentedly under the curls at a girl's neck while she bisected squids in the laboratory; and parakeets hopped about on living-room pictures and mantels. Food began to disappear in large amounts from dining rooms and kitchen. The cooks objected in no uncertain language and threatened to quit. Maids gave notice, declaring that they had not "hired out to scrub kennels." The trustees complained that the costly shrubs and perennials which had been planted with such loving care had begun to wither and die, and brown spots dotted the beautiful lawns. Everyone looked to the administration to pass a law. But the president only smiled patiently and said that it was up to the students to deal with the problem.

Then the "thing" finally occurred that had been prophesied not only by cautious faculty members but by critics of the college up and down the land. An instructor who lived with his wife in an apartment under one of the student suites was aroused late one cold November night by a wailing, like the cry of a newborn infant. He was still shaky when he told about it the next morning. "I sat up listening," he said, "but my heart thumped so hard that I could hardly hear anything else. It happened again—that plaintive wail—there was no mistaking it! I groped for the telephone to call the doctor but decided I'd better arouse my wife first. 'Wake up!' I said, grabbing and shaking her. 'For God's sake, wake up—it's happened at last!' We crept upstairs and tiptoed down the hall to the girl's room. Everything was still, except that incessant crying. My wife pushed open the door gingerly and switched on the light. And, so help me, there was that girl, Amy, curled up on the bed with her head buried under a pillow, dead to the world! Over by the open window, a lambkin shivered and stared at us forlornly and kept crying, 'Ma —ma—maaa.' My wife had a good laugh but I was damn disgusted. This pet nuisance has gone too far!"

The students, too, were up in arms. They hadn't relished the implications of the incident. Worried dog owners hastened to build wire fences around the base of trees and shrubs. The lambkin was returned to the farm from which it had been purloined; the cats and their hungry litters were doled out to the town's children. Only the parakeets and the white mice stayed on as reminders of the heyday of Bennington's pets. But the president's faith in the ability of the students to handle their problems had been vindicated. They passed an all-time rule forbidding pets on the campus. And so the college's first tradition began to take root.

Bennington was an endless adventure in learning for faculty and staff as well as for students. We were all in a continuous process of fermentation. The most enlightening experiences for me were in the weekly meetings of the Student Personnel Committee, of which I was chairman. In addition, the membership included President Leigh, the college physician, the director of records, a teacher chosen at large by the student body, and the counselors of the two or three undergraduates whose progress, or lack of it, was being considered. A secretary took the minutes and summed up the comments and suggestions for filing in the individual folders.

During the year every girl's program, including her extracurricular activities, was scrutinized and changes in trial majors and counselors approved when advisable. It was the aim of the committee to make recommendations and adjustments that would enable the good student to do better and the failing one to overcome some of her difficulties. The educational plan was tested ruthlessly to determine where it fell short in meeting the undergraduate's needs; and revisions when necessary were brought to a faculty vote. The college actually evolved out of the discussions and decisions in this vital committee. The trial-major system, a device for helping the student in her first two years to discover her real bent, was continuously probed for its effectiveness. Counselors began to re-appraise the capabilities of their "counselees" and instructors were led to examine their own methods.

I had banked heavily on the presence of the psychiatrist as a member of the Student Personnel Committee. Here my naïveté had led me astray. I had seen Dr. Ebaugh only by appointment, never in a situation where he was individually involved. I had sometimes misunderstood his detachment and refusal to give me detailed instructions as to how to proceed in dealing with a student's problem. It would have been so easy, it seemed, for him to lift the entire burden from my shoulders. But instead he schooled me in a few basic principles of mental hygiene and sent me back to my job to use my own insight and intelligence. Now and then I had rebelled against what appeared to be his indifference, but here, a decade later, the reason was becoming clear. It occurred to me that the psychiatrist, as a scientist, needed to fight continuously for perspective and a degree of solitude. He suffered the emotional ups and downs that were the common lot. And often there might have been a conflict of such severity that it drove him—as it had driven Dr. Ebaugh—into the profession of medicine and psychiatry to find the cause and cure of his own affliction.

Bennington's doctor was trying to fill an impossible position. Her apartment adjoined her office in the Commons building, where she had neither privacy nor solitude. She gave so unsparingly of her time that she often became irritable and short-tempered. Undoubtedly she did a great deal of good about which no one except the persons concerned ever knew. But some students who might have benefited most from her counsel claimed that she was prejudiced and often unjust. These varied shades of feeling, ranging from antipathy to blind worship, even crept into the meetings of the Student Personnel Committee and sometimes threatened to create friction. In the end, however, the doctor was usually deferred to, out of respect for her greater knowledge, experience, and personal integrity.

But I began to question the advisability of having a full-time, resident psychiatrist on the staff of a small college. It would be better to install her off campus in the town, it seemed, where she would be available for consultation or a series of lectures to faculty and students—and where listeners could not glimpse the cracks in her armor. The frank revelations in the committee changed some of my other ideas, this time about my own work. I came to realize the unreliability of the hit-and-miss aptitude scores which had been used as part of the admissions procedure.

Frequently earlier doubts as to the validity of "special interests" had proved justified. A few students, usually those talented in science or the arts, had known definitely what they wanted to study and stood by it throughout the course. But many others had merely been indulging in daydreams. One who declared passionately that she wanted to be a writer failed consistently in English composition. It turned out that she had been trying to follow in the footsteps of an idolized aunt who was a noted author. The zealous ichthyologist who yearned to write her Doctor's thesis someday on the "Fishes of Boston Harbor" had settled for a bowl of goldfish in her room and was concentrating in the field of music. Elizabeth, the amateur carpenter, had discovered her niche in the biological laboratory where she was doing very well on the anatomy of cats. The whole student body, it seemed, was in a state of intellectual agitation and often the counselors grew restive, waiting for the happy end of the long honeymoon.

Occasionally I went to one of the student lounges after lunch in the Commons and watched the dancing. I was certain, in spite of some of the disturbing testimony at the Student Personnel meetings, that no college in the country could boast of a prettier, more graceful and interesting group of freshman girls. The thought that I had known them all before and had played a small part in bringing them together for the exciting venture on that beautiful Vermont campus gave me a sense of satisfaction and joy that I had seldom, if ever, experienced.

XVII

In view of Bennington's location in the
Green Mountains, some distance from cultural centers such as
those found in Boston and New York, the college administration felt it important to provide a place in its program for distinguished speakers from the outside and exponents of the arts.
Martha Graham, the choreographer and dance idol of young
moderns, was among the first to be invited. The third floor of
the Commons, which was used for all assembly purposes, shook
dangerously with the applause and stamping feet that followed
her recital. It was fertile soil for Martha Graham's genius. She
seemed to feel at her best before a youthful audience that understood and loved her art and returned again and again for hardly
any fees, not only to dance but to aid Martha Hill in the development of such a department at the college.

Scarcely a month passed without a fine exhibition of paintings, sculpture, or artifacts; and the best string ensembles and
well-known vocal, piano, and violin artists appeared at intervals
to move the campus with great music. On Friday night there
was usually a lecture by some famous literary figure, like Archi-
bald MacLeish, whose epic poem *Conquistador* had recently
been published, or Dorothy Canfield Fisher and Julia Peterkin,
the novelists, or Margaret Mead, the anthropologist. But the

students seemed to like best to hear Carl Sandburg singing his simple lyric poems, accompanying himself on a guitar; or Robert Frost and his neighborly poetry about his adopted homeland in Vermont.

It was inevitable that e. e. cummings, the noted poet who usually scorned punctuation and the use of capital letters even for his own name, should one day hear the call of Bennington College. He was known as a non-conformist in every respect and the students deified him together with Martha Graham. They knew most of his poems by heart and had set some of them to their contrapuntal music. As if his creations were not enough, it was said that he had the face and build of a movie star! Little else was talked about for days before his scheduled appearance.

People from town stood around the walls of the big room in the Commons, unable to get seats. The atmosphere was tense and expectant; the applause as he stepped to the podium grew deafening. He smiled and bowed appreciatively and began to turn the pages of a small book. A second's hush fell upon the crowd, and then, suddenly, the students in one voice began to chant:

> *buffalo bill's*
> *defunct*
> > *who used to*
> > *ride a watersmooth-silver*
> > > *stallion*
> *and break onetwothreefourfive pigeons justlike that*
> > > > > *Jesus*
>
> *he was a handsome man*
> > > > *and what i want to know is*
> *how do you like your blueeyed boy*
> *Mister Death*

From the stress on the seventh and eighth lines of the poem it was very evident that the students were paying a tribute to estlin cummings, not Buffalo Bill. A broad grin spread over his face before he was able to recapture the mood for his readings. It was a thrilling moment for the girls but there were outside repercussions. News of the incident spread through the quiet countryside and shocked the good people with its seeming irreverence. What were things coming to, they said, when the name of the Lord was held up to ridicule in the name of art! The pastors of the area were especially concerned and protested to the president. But he seemed as amused by the students' spontaneous salute as the poet himself had been. He also expressed annoyance at the persistent criticisms from the clergy taking him to task for not providing for religious instruction in the Bennington Plan.

The matter reached a climax when a large group of New England ministers invited him to speak at an annual meeting in Hartford, Connecticut. They reminded him that the idea of a college in Bennington had first been conceived by their respected colleague, Dr. Vincent Ravi-Booth, and the members were anxious to know what provision was being made to enrich the spiritual life of the young students. It was reported, they went on, that no plans were being considered for building a chapel, or even to set aside a "meditation room," and that the Holy Bible was to be studied only as great literature. Would President Leigh be so kind as to throw some light on the evident misconceptions and allay the serious concern of their parishioners?

He came by my office as he was preparing to leave in his faded blue Buick car. "I declare," he said, "I haven't been able to sleep for nights, thinking about the ordeal ahead. I've wondered what I could say beyond the statement that Mrs. Leigh and I and our two daughters are faithful members of the Old

First Congregational Church in Old Bennington and that the college students will be encouraged to affiliate with their own denominations. "But I am determined," he went on, "to resist every pressure to commit the college to any one creed or set of creeds!"

There was a streak of opportunism in him that often rescued him when pushed into a corner. Even as he spoke, I detected a certain gleam in his eyes, the same one I had noticed once before when he blithely turned over the problem of pets to the students for solution. I wondered what he was going to say to the ministers. He seemed particularly lighthearted after returning from the meeting and I couldn't restrain my curiosity. "How did the conference turn out?" I asked, trying to appear casual.

"Great! It was a fine group of clergymen and I think they will be more understanding of our program from now on."

"What did you tell them?"

"Well, sir, I got an idea as I was pulling into Hartford. It saved the situation. I decided to dump the whole matter into the preachers' laps. If they would appoint a committee to draw up a proposal for religious instruction, I said, one that would be consistent with the rest of the plan, and acceptable to our faculty and Board of Trustees, it would be given earnest consideration." He smiled reminiscently. "I believe they saw the reasonableness of the suggestion and were impressed by the college's willingness to co-operate. To tell the truth, though, I doubt if we'll ever hear anything more of it. You see, our Board of Trustees, of which Dr. Ravi-Booth is a member, has been puzzling over this dilemma for years and has never been able to find the right answer. But hereafter the ministers will have to share the brunt of the criticism and maybe they will come up, at last, with a solution."

Apparently his remarks had won increased confidence. Interest in the college, which, so far, had been centered mainly in the East, had spread across the country to the West Coast. It was decided that I should use the months of January and February, coinciding with the Winter Field and Reading Period, for a long journey of interviewing and visiting schools. I looked forward to the experience with great enthusiasm. Now I would have something more tangible to talk about than charts and maps punctuated by a red barn, a chicken coop, and a meadow full of wild flowers. Furthermore, the disciplining sessions in the Student Personnel Committee had taught me a few valuable lessons, especially about the tricky admissions requirement called "special interests." I was not going to be misled any more, but would seek dedicated students like Lorie who planned to devote her life to doing research into a disease of turkeys called "blackhead."

It was going to be a wrench to leave my cozy home in the Hall House. This was my own dream come true and I wanted to put down roots and stay forever. My few cherished possessions had not been unpacked since I left Bemis Hall. Seeing them again was like meeting old friends; the living room seemed to have been waiting for them. The painting of a Japanese junk, on uncut velvet—a wedding gift to Howe and me—was just right for the wall above the fireplace. The mantelpiece made a colorful setting for the Orrefors decanter, a memento of my summer with the Alkmans in Sweden; the blue-green Van Briggle vase brought from Colorado Springs; and the Florentine glass bowl, fringed with delicate flowers, which Maria Loschi, the Italian countess, had sent me after her visit. Everything in the apartment seemed to have a special meaning for me, from the white-painted shelves filled with my own books to the early American center table topped with an enchanting photograph of Barbara in a silver frame.

She had finished her year at the Yale School of Drama, where she studied playwriting and directing under the noted George

Pierce Baker, and was now living in New York, trying to get a
foothold in the theater, along with numerous other young hope-
fuls. The competition was rough and discouraging, but she
never seemed disheartened. I was grateful to give her a lift,
figuring that, by rights, she should have had two more years of
college. And there was always her own room in my apartment
where she came occasionally to spend weekends, and to bring
me up-to-date on her adventures. Lately she had begun to get
small parts in such radio programs as "Gangbusters" and "The
March of Time," and a soap opera called "Portia Faces Life."
We couldn't have been more thrilled if she were playing in *Biography*, the current hit at the Theatre Guild!

The first Christmas in our new home was a real celebration.
The college was almost deserted, with all the students off for
the holidays and then going on their various field projects which
would occupy them for the next six weeks. Most of the faculty
members, too, had departed to do reading in metropolitan libraries, attend some of the latest plays and concerts, and take
in the current art exhibits in New York and Boston galleries.
But Irving Fineman, my next-door neighbor, had stayed in Bennington to work on a novel. We invited him to dinner, and,
although Prohibition was still a law, he managed somewhere to
find a bottle of sparkling burgundy to liven the party. The week
came to an end all too soon for me. Barbara's agent had called
her back to New York, and I was getting ready to leave for
Chicago where I had an engagement to speak at a luncheon of
the Fortnightly Club.

Deep snow lay on the ground the day I left, and icicles hung
from the eaves of the station in North Bennington, giving the
village the look of a Christmas card. It was pleasant to think
that shortly I would be spending a few weeks in the land of
palms and mockingbirds. It seemed unlikely, just then, that anything I might say about the advantages of attending Bennington

College would ever lure students away from the sub-tropical charms of Stanford University. But as I neared the field of conquest my old zest returned. I pictured the informal, homelike living rooms and the pastel tinted suites in the small student residences. The close proximity of Williams College was given special emphasis, in the hope of compensating for Bennington's lack of men. I indulged in a bit of boasting about the quality of the faculty, the tutorial system, and superior counseling. Now some of the accomplishments of the beginning students could be described—the murals painted in a corridor of the Barn; the two large granite squirrels being sculptured by a Boston girl to mark either side of the pathway leading down the hill to the Commons; the dance compositions presented in recital by pupils of Martha Hill; and the music of dissonant scales floating up from the studios in the revamped Chicken Coop.

It still made a wonderful story, in my opinion, but few high school seniors or parents went so far as to ask for application blanks. I had forgotten that my paeans were about an institution with radically different ideas of education. I had come to some of the most conservative sections in the country. Many of the early settlers were still living and contented with things as they were and always had been. They feared change and grew suspicious of outsiders who came from the East or North to tell them how to educate their children. Besides, they said, they wanted their boys and girls to go to colleges nearer home where they would be among their friends. I could not help sympathizing with these sentiments. My own western college still had a firm hold on my loyalty.

But southerners, who often valued the social graces for their daughters more than intellectual attainments, were impressed by rumors that Bennington's first class had been composed mostly of debutantes from wealthy, influential New York and Boston families. They were amazed when I told them that some of these "debutantes" had come from Depression-poor backgrounds and were glad enough to earn part of their expenses by waiting on table in the college dining rooms or cleaning the apartments of faculty members. Even so, parents did not go so far as to make application; they, too, seemed to have grown more guarded.

My most dramatic experience happened unexpectedly in Charleston, South Carolina. I had been speaking at one of the most exclusive private schools for girls in the South when one of the teachers asked me if I would be interested in visiting the large high school for Negro boys and girls. I was delighted with the opportunity and she arranged with the principal for me to talk at the assembly the following morning. President Leigh and I had often discussed the possibility of admitting a well-qualified Negro student to Bennington College, and now it seemed as if the chance might come. Among so many, I thought hopefully, there would surely be one girl who could be considered. I was eager to talk it over with the principal.

He was a fine-looking man with a reserved and courteous manner. I sat beside him on the platform, looking into a sea of dark, expectant faces. How still the room was! Not a sound could be heard, not a cough nor a foot scraping. Then a young woman stepped to the front, struck a chord once or twice on the piano, and signaled with her baton. All of a sudden, hundreds of full, rich voices broke into "Swing Low, Sweet Chariot." Never before had I heard it sung so beautifully. Almost without a pause, it was followed by "Deep River" and "Steal Away to Jesus." They closed with the moving spiritual, "Were You There?" The words lingered in my memory:

> "*Were you there*
> *When they crucified my Lord?*
> *Were you there*
> *When they crucified my Lord?*
> *Oh! Sometimes it causes me to tremble, tremble, tremble.*
> *Were you there when they crucified my Lord?*"

The music poured from their hearts as if they were singing to me alone. And when at last I got up to speak, my voice choked for a moment and my eyes filled with tears. Never before had Bennington College seemed so far away. I knew, as I scanned the faces, that no Negro girl could afford to go there, no matter how fine her school record nor how large the reduction in the tuition fee, for nowhere had the Depression struck deeper than among southern Negroes.

It was April when I returned to the campus. The four new student houses were nearing completion and the second semester was in full swing. A fine clock, the gift of Miss Mary Sanford, tolled the hours from the Commons tower. My work, too, had gained momentum. Twice as many applications as there had been the year before were waiting to be considered. The president had given me a great deal of freedom in making what we called "on-the-spot" selections, and already a number of candidates whose qualifications were outstanding had been admitted during my school visits. The class began to fill up rapidly in the next few months, and, as it neared completion, we were able to start a waiting list. When college opened in the fall, every room had been assigned, without even a cranny for doubles!

And this was the year that Lorie arrived, with several crates of sick gobblers!

The superintendent of buildings and grounds hastily put up a wire enclosure for the turkeys, just below the Chicken Coop now housing the music studios. Faculty members seemed greatly impressed by the scholarly young girl, and their compliments caused me to puff out with pride. This was the admissions system running in high, I said to myself, with the throttle wide open for all the world to hear! I little realized how soon it would turn out to be literally true. The birds gobbled incessantly as if trying to compete with the pianos, violins, and double bassoons practicing harmonics in the old henhouse. Instructors didn't complain when their classes were disturbed, saying that they were willing to make any sacrifice for the sake of medical science.

But after a week or two some of the students concluded that the turkeys were suffering from malnutrition and hunger rather than liver complaints, and they began to sneak food for them from the dining rooms and kitchen. Lorie seemed vaguely unconcerned, even when the birds' hackles drooped and their wattles grew paler and paler. She had a dreamy look in her pretty blue eyes akin to homesickness. Then one morning an ominous quiet settled over the campus. The turkeys had flown the coop!

Excitement was rampant. What had become of the sick and half-starved fowls? Lorie had overslept, and one of the students hurried to waken her, saying that her biology teacher wanted to see her at once. Such conferences were usually confidential, but the story leaked out that she confessed to knowing nothing about the care of turkeys. Her well-to-do father, it was said, had always hired a man for this kind of work at their country place outside of Boston. But one November just before Thanksgiving several of the blooded gobblers died of some mysterious ailment called "blackhead." Lorie was only sixteen and deeply impressionable. She resolved then and there to devote her time, when she went to college, to studying the cause and cure of this fowl disease. Apparently I arrived on the scene at just the opportune moment, bringing her tidings of the new college in Vermont where she could pursue her burning interest.

Meanwhile, the villagers reported seeing the strange birds as far away as Green's Corners. One handsome young fellow, who lived on a small farm over in the valley, inquired about the owner and took the trouble to crate and haul some of them in his truck back to the enclosure below the Chicken Coop. Evidently he was touched by her inexperience with barnyard creatures and returned several evenings in a row to teach her the rudiments. The next thing the community knew, Lorie was missing. She and the farmer had eloped!

XVIII

"*Life* is like many rivers flowing along, continuously modifying and shaping their banks," Dr. Kilpatrick had said at one of the early community meetings. "So it is with human beings. No individual here tonight will be the same when she leaves this room as when she entered. My words alone will not have changed her. Countless other forces will have left their invisible marks, altering and molding her character for the mysterious course ahead. It is well to be aware of this ceaseless process going on within and outside each one of us and to learn how to accept, adapt to and direct it for the best possible purpose."

Nowhere was the attrition more pronounced than in the discussions of the Committee on Student Personnel. It was here that differences of opinion and conviction were aired. "The program is over-individualized. Too much emphasis is being placed on self-interests," one counselor said, "resulting in a lack of social concern." "We are failing in one of the chief aims for which the college was founded," another agreed, "the development of social responsibility." He cited the case of Mary, one of his brightest counselees, who was so dedicated to art that she wanted to spend her whole time with oils and brushes up in the studio. She never went to community meetings nor attended parties. Even her recreation was taken alone, driving to neighboring villages, painting whatever struck her fancy. All sorts of devices, he continued, in a tone of frustration, had been contrived to turn Mary at least into a part-time extrovert. And she had co-operated nobly, but as soon as the collective back was turned, she withdrew again into her preoccupation with painting land-scapes. "For God's sake, let's leave her alone," another counselor spoke up in exasperation, "in my opinion we're putting alto-gether too much stress on group consciousness."

Many serious weaknesses became apparent in the trial-major system. Often, it seemed, students flitted through the curriculum sampling subjects, like butterflies looking for a soft spot on which to rest. There was talk of requiring a basic core of studies for all students in the Junior Division. Everybody, including the president, came in for criticism. Teachers were not always the best counselors, it was said; some of them had no interest what-ever in a girl's emotional problems. They had to be reminded that their job was to "teach students, not subjects." Again, the president was accused of occasionally forgetting democratic pro-cedures in dealing with an urgent situation and behaved like a dictator-dean. Somewhere the voice of the psychiatrist could be heard trying to guide conflicting opinions toward intelligent so-lutions. But now and then she too went overboard and suffered a loss of authority, such as the night of the impromptu faculty party when the repeal of Prohibition was celebrated with ex-cessive zeal. Amateur psychoanalysts burgeoned all over the campus and often by-passed the college physician in their at-tempts to straighten out the quirks of a disturbed member of the group. The unhappy victim was not always a freshman. There was Sylvia for instance, the well-to-do wife of an instructor. She was unusually competent and had a great deal of executive abil-ity that was going to waste. Unfortunately, no position on the staff was available and she became a problem to herself as well as to the faculty. Some of us fondly conspired together and persuaded her to be analyzed by one of New York's famous psychiatrists. The suggestion evidently beguiled her—a warning which we should have heeded!

She made the weekly trip to the city all winter and was seldom seen around the campus halls. We congratulated ourselves for having been so astute and looked forward to her return to the Bennington fold, with everything under control. But we were destined for a sharp awakening. It didn't take long to discover that Sylvia was the same restless, meddlesome woman she had been before analysis; she hadn't changed in the slightest degree. And worse still, she now knew exactly what ailed all the rest of us!

The Winter Field and Reading Period—soon called the Winter Period—developed into one of the most successful features of the Bennington Plan. President Leigh had told me, rather modestly, the day we had our first interview that it had been his own innovation. "I never liked cold, snowy weather," he said, "and for several years have taken my family and gone to Florida for a few weeks around Christmas. One day when I was trying to figure out a way to escape Vermont's midwinter blizzards, the idea came to me of instituting a period away from the campus for six or eight weeks when everybody would have the opportunity to travel, or work in metropolitan libraries, or even take apprentice jobs in the line of one's interest. It may take some organization and co-operation in the beginning but ultimately it should become an essential part of our program."

It was lucky that he happened to be in faraway Palm Beach that first winter when Bennington turned its girls loose on an unsuspecting world, to pursue whatever projects their counselors could improvise. Some hurried home, in order to save expense, and killed time reading in local libraries; others made social debuts which they claimed had "great educational value." A few went traveling to Washington, London, and Geneva "to observe national and international affairs." Still others did volunteer duties in settlement houses in Chicago, New York, and Boston. One or two acted as messengers in publishing firms, or sat in on meetings of buyers at fashionable specialty shops on Fifth Avenue "to determine style trends." The best that could be said for the initial experiment was that it broke the isolation of rural Vermont and threw the girls into a healthy association with men.

As time progressed and organization improved, however, the Winter Period began to show such promise that it was planned to engage a full-time director of the non-resident term. Projects were arranged more carefully to tie in with the student's college program. Excellent reports came back from employees and supervisors, praising the contributions of the girls and their earnestness in trying to learn a few of the fundamentals of a job. Some even offered to give them positions as soon as they had finished their education. It made a dramatic story for me to tell in my visits to high schools across the country, especially the one about Ruth, the closely sheltered daughter of a Harvard professor.

Students whose field experience had been unusually interesting were always invited to speak at assembly meetings soon after the opening of the spring term. Ruth was among the unforgettables. New England reserve was reflected in her quiet brown eyes and rather shy manner. By no stretch of the imagination could one see her as a day laborer. But Ruth's major in college was economics and she intended to concentrate on the problems of women in industry. Someday she hoped to become a professional arbitrator in labor disputes. Her first Winter Period was spent as a worker in a big dress factory in Fall River, Massachusetts, where most of the employees were young girls. In order to get the job, she had changed her name, accent, and way of dressing; and to win the confidence of the others, she carried a meager lunch, chewed gum, and entered into the talk about "bosses," inspectors, the "old man," and boy friends.

"To my amazement," she said, in speaking at the college assembly, "most of the girls were barely seventeen years old and often they were the main support of their families. Sometimes four or five members lived in one tenement room, without hot and cold running water and only one toilet to a floor. When a girl's boy friend wanted to see her, they had to walk the streets or huddle in hallways. It wasn't unusual to find her mother and the "old man" in a drunken fight when she came back from the day's work, and all her week's wages spent on beer! I had to remind myself constantly," she went on, "that, but for the grace of God, I might have been any one of them." The students, as they listened to her closing remarks, were as still as death. "I have come back to Bennington a humbler person. Never again will I look upon human beings in quite the same way. And I am determined to do what I can toward improving working conditions and making a better life possible for the working people of our country."

Students like Ruth, and many others going out to widely scattered work assignments, invariably gave a fine impression of the new college and made it comparatively easy to secure the full, four-year student body. It was only yesterday, it seemed, when the first houses welcomed the bevy of hand-picked girls. Now, three years after, 300 undergraduates quickened the campus and enlivened the twelve attractive residences bordering the Green. In spite of being almost grown up, Bennington suffered the tragedies and mistakes that afflict human beings wherever they collect, in villages, towns, and on college grounds. There had been deaths and divorces to sadden and disturb the community. Some teachers had left and others came to take their places. Too many students had dropped out or failed to make the difficult passage from Junior to Senior Divisions.

The process of leavening went on, however, experimenting, changing, testing. Three vital Educational Policies Committees were organized, one appointed from among the trustees, another representing the faculty, and the third elected by students in the major departments of the Senior Division. The scrutiny, criticism, and suggestions of these co-operating groups helped further to unravel the tangled skeins of the curriculum and added threads to strengthen the weak spots.

My particular concern, along with admissions, was with the Community Government, whose membership included everyone in the college, from the president to the superintendent of buildings and grounds. Matters of conduct were considered by the Central Committee, made up of a group of elected students, the registrar, and the director of admissions. The staff members were not there as "deans" or "wardens" but rather as observers and older counselors. The rules were largely specific campus laws. Nothing was said about when to go to bed and turn off the lights. Noise was discouraged after eleven o'clock. Evenings spent off campus had no strings attached. A girl was supposed to sign out if she expected to stay after eleven and sign in when she returned. A night officer on duty at the entrance to the residential area kept out intruders and gave the girls keys to their various houses. Because of the distance from other towns and cities, no issue was made of frequent weekends away from the college, provided the student's work didn't suffer.

Early in the fall of 1932, the following two standards were proposed and adopted by the students and faculty: 1) Members of the Bennington College community shall always conduct themselves in an orderly manner, respecting the regulations of any community in which they may be; and 2) Every member of the community shall conduct himself as a responsible citizen in constructive co-operation with the college and its aims. These standards were both firm and flexible enough to give leeway for the individual interpretation of infractions of the rules which had to be dealt with by the Central Committee. The unwritten theme of Community Government was "Freedom with Responsibility." Violations of the standards and rules were inevitable, especially after the repeal of Prohibition when cocktail and sherry parties became respectable customs. But as I looked back over the years of living and working among college women, it seemed to me that the problems of behavior were less serious than they were when the Dean of Women lived "in residence," combining the duties of arbiter of good taste with those of a "prestigious policewoman." And the attitude toward errant individuals and the ways of dealing with their misconduct had undergone radical change. The techniques of mental hygiene were no longer *sub rosa* in practice. The better colleges did not apologize for referring "cases" to a consulting psychiatrist; and student self-government organizations had become honestly independent.

There was something about Bennington College, over and above the educational plan, that enriched the human spirit, no matter whether the stay lasted a few months or several years. The president once described it in an assembly talk as "a place of spontaneous good humor and joyous living." He spoke of the "subtle stabilizing influence" which daily contact with nature and rural scenes provided and of the "friendliness and democracy" that prevailed in everyday life. It was a place where exposure of sham and artificiality spared no one; a soil where young people of any age had been freed to bear whatever fruit or flower was in their nature to yield. And it was a haven for perennial youth. No inert ideas withered on the stem for want of expression; no musty traditions cluttered the archives. The present and the future, with only a glance backward now and then, were all important. "Start from where you are and go forward" might have been the motto if Bennington had not scoffed such trite maxims.

Time was no respecter of persons and it had moved me along at frightening speed, together with the growing college. Already I was the oldest living relic of the early days. Already it was June 1936, and the campus was in a flutter of excitement over the first Commencement. Parents and visitors in summer clothes were swarming over the hillside and crowding into the square in front of the Barn where the exercises were to be held. Surely, I said to myself, this is the strangest of all my commencements! No college colors marked off the section where the fifty seniors would sit. Indeed, Bennington had never got around to choosing any colors; they were not considered suitable for its tradition-scorning character. No programs were passed around giving the order of the ceremonies and listing the names of students who had won honors. In fact, there was no honor system because the grades on which it was based had no place in the academic plan. No distinguished speaker from the outside had been invited to address the students. The occasion was a family affair, warm, informal, and intimate.

At first, I missed the dignified procession of the Board of Trustees and faculty members, in academic regalia, marching slowly down the aisle. Instead, they were scattered through the audience just like ordinary people. Barbara had come up from New York to be with me for the event and I found myself wishing, for her sake, that Bennington College for this brief hour might make a bow to pomp and circumstance and that somewhere the strains of Guilmant's *Triumphal March* could be heard as President Leigh and Dr. Vincent Ravi-Booth preceded the seniors, in Alice-blue gowns and skull caps, to their places in the two front rows. But these were rituals worn threadbare with the ages and Bennington belonged to the modern era.

The base of the old silo served as a platform where the president and Dr. Ravi-Booth sat in their academic robes—the one concession to custom. The president riffled through his notes for the short inspirational talk to the class while the pastor of Old Bennington's Old First Congregational Church smiled absently as he looked out upon the large gathering. This was the realization of his dream for an educational center for girls in that lovely corner of Vermont. After a decade of devotion and hope and endless hours of work, the vision had taken form. One could only imagine what his thoughts and feelings had been when he rose slowly to pronounce the benediction.

Suddenly, at the conclusion, the music of strange pastoral instruments began to flow from the upper windows of the Barn and I saw Elizabeth, the amateur carpenter now a major in biology, directing a group of bell ringers in a Bach chorale. It was the most beautiful sound I had ever heard! How little I had realized that day I had hesitated about admitting the girl with the "quiet, intelligent eyes" that she would contribute so much to the character and spirit of the new college!

As we got up to leave, I turned to Barbara, half seeking a sign of wistfulness or regret that she was not among the graduates. Perhaps she would still consider entering the college. Age was no handicap, already several older girls had been admitted. When I saw no indication that she had changed her mind, I pressed the question, "What did you think of Bennington's first Commencement?"

Almost as if not seeing me, she said with a faint smile, "Oh— it was fine, Mother—just fine——" She turned away and I realized that her thoughts had filled the scene with other meanings and her own drama—to my daughter this would always be an alien cast; only the world of the theater claimed her heart.

Driving back from Albany late that night, after taking her to the train for New York, I found myself drifting in reverie over the long years since Howe's death. Nothing had ever healed the

scar of loneliness. Other wounds, too, had been callused over
only to give me a twinge of pain, in retrospect. It seemed incredible that I had never re-married but as I progressed in my
profession I seemed to have lost a certain romantic appeal for
men. Or perhaps I had required more of them in the way of
companionship and intellectual congeniality. I suspected that po-
tential husbands shied away from women who might demand
too much of them; they did not relish the possibility of giving
up their independent bachelor habits. And gradually I had begun to cherish my own freedom.

But on this wonderful day, a warm sense of reconciliation
with fate had come to me. My daughter had found her niche
and the future for her showed promise. We were grownup
friends, at last, with affection and respect for each other's individuality. Soon there would be time for me to start writing
again—some pieces about Sweden—several articles on the new
developments in the education of women. Then I should start
organizing my large collection of notes for the long-planned
book about the gold rush years in Cripple Creek. What a full
and interesting life beckoned ahead!

It was well after midnight when I reached the turn in the
road that led past the Colgate mansion and down the grade a
short distance to the Hall House. Darkness blotted out the
countryside, but the light in the driveway by my door was shining a welcome. It had been a long and memorable day; for the
first time I was overcome with weariness. How good it was to
be home!

Postscript

It was April 1957. Twenty-five years had passed since the opening day of Bennington College. Much water had flowed under the bridge and, in spite of the hopes and prayers of mankind, some of it had been stained by the blood of the Second World War and a war in Korea. The Great Depression had vanished and in its wake came something even worse called the "Cold War." All the prosperity in the land could not abolish our festering hatreds and fears of Russian communism nor stay the race for atomic missiles.

Time was running its natural course with me. I had long since retired from colleges and their dormitories. After a brief, disillusioning spell of war work in Washington, I moved to California where Barbara had gone to live after her marriage. My small pension was scarcely equal to the soaring cost of mere existence, but in one thing I was rich—there was plenty of leisure for writing. The specter of old age hovered over me; already I had used up my allotment of three score and ten and had lost self-confidence. But with encouragement from Lowell Thomas, once my pupil in a Cripple Creek high school, I set about putting together the voluminous notes I had made about the gold-rush years of that famous old mining camp.

I was working on a rough draft of the seventh chapter of the book when a surprising letter came that was destined to fill my

life with miraculous new experiences. It was from Fletcher in
Denver, one of the girls in Bennington's first class. I remembered her well—her laughter always rippling near the surface,
her young vitality and infectious idealism. She had written
to ask if I were going to attend the May celebration of the
twenty-fifth anniversary of the college's opening. I had thought
about it, of course, but making such a long trip was out of
the question. She must have anticipated my reply for she
went on to say that if I hadn't already made plans, some of
the girls would like to have me come as their guest. "We
hope you'll accept our invitation," she said; "it wouldn't be
quite the same without you."

It must have been a kind of conspiracy for almost in the next
mail another letter came, this one from Emelea in Washington,
enclosing a generous check and urging me to accept it. Even
so, I hesitated. It seemed too much for the students to do. Also,
perhaps a little streak of vanity possessed me. Bennington, to
me, was still the perennial youngling; I might look like a left-
over from the Middle Ages. Then it occurred to me that I had
gone back to my own Golden Jubilee at Colorado College, only
the year before, and had had a wonderful time meeting old
friends and classmates. The new president was a vigorous, im-
aginative person who had charted a modern course for the college, with many fine buildings to bring it in line with the best
institutions in the country. Bemis Hall, as prim and dignified as
ever, was about to yield some of her prestige to a beautiful residence for women students called Loomis Hall. I was grateful
as I strolled over the familiar campus that, by some incredible
chance, I had been an undergraduate there, and later, by another switch of fate, had returned against my will to be re-
educated as its Dean of Women. The renewal of old times had
been refreshing. I wouldn't have missed it——

A feeling of affection stole over me as I read Emmie's letter again. I wondered how high the ivy had reached on the east wall of the Commons, flaunting its shiny leaves in the face of tradition. The student houses by now must have that lived-in, settled look that I came to love in New England homes. And the Hall House—the bittersweet vine I had planted by my front door must be clinging to the eaves! A gay procession of radiant, youthful girls began to move across my memory. Hannah, the violinist; scholarly Yvette; Asho of the happy nature; Isabella, the sculptress; and Lillias with the twinkly eyes—now her father had become Secretary of State. How good it would be to see them, and all the others who had become my dear friends! I would write Emmie at once—no—I would telephone her that very evening!

It was Barbara who suggested, as I was packing my bags, that I take along a few chapters and the outline of my book. "You might as well go down to New York," she said, "and perhaps Lowell could put you in touch with a good publisher." I still nursed a vague dread of New York but, even so, I took her advice and set out in high spirits, by plane, for one of the most heartening adventures of my life.

The campus, always loveliest in May, had put on its leafiest show. I hardly recognized it with the tall lacy elms shading the Green and the full-grown buddleia and forsythia bushes bursting with violet and yellow blossoms. Hundreds of graduates and former students, together with many of the original faculty members, had come back for the occasion. Most of the girls were married; some had brought their husbands and children. One or two boasted of having daughters enrolled in the college. I managed to steal away for a glimpse of Hall House. Strange tenants occupied the apartments, and the greedy bittersweet vine had been uprooted. Instructors had been moved to attractive cottages on the campus or in near-by North Bennington. The old road up past the graveyard had been abandoned as the entrance, and

beautiful iron gates marked the winding highway which led to
the main buildings. The Barn with its white trim and nostalgic
appeal still held its own as the center of administration, but the
fast-growing library had inched its way through an entire wing
of the ground floor. The Chicken Coop no longer resounded
with musical discords; the studios had taken over "Fairview," the
beautiful mansion willed to the college by Mrs. Jennings at her
death.

A program of lectures, concerts, and seminars led by faculty
members had been planned for our pleasure and enlightenment.
We learned that the happy hunting days of "trial majoring"
were over and that Junior Division students were required to
take certain basic courses referred to as General Education. Two
presidents had succeeded Dr. Leigh, and lo and behold, a Dean
of the college had been appointed! But as yet there was no Dean
of Women, only an attractive, competent individual known as
the director of student personnel. Bennington College had out-
grown its adolescent years and had reached its majority as a respected member of the best American colleges for women. Other
institutions had adopted modifications of some of its successful
experiments, especially in admissions and the extended Winter
Field and Reading Period; and Bennington had toned down
some of its more radical innovations and become slightly conservative.

It was hard to say good-by at last and to turn my lingering
eyes from the scene. It wasn't likely that I would ever return,
or see again many of the young friends who had brought so
much happiness to my life. But I was too grateful for the wonder of that weekend to find room in my heart for sorrow.

I had sent Lowell a note telling him of my trip to Bennington, and he telephoned, inviting me to spend a few days with
him and Mrs. Thomas at their home in Pawling. He had already arranged an appointment for me with "one of the finest

editors in New York," Ken McCormick at Doubleday. I bought a new brief case for the occasion and filled it with my precious cargo. It seemed unreal to find myself, after almost a lifetime of dreaming and hoping, face to face with the editor who held my fate in his hands. But his pleasant, relaxed manner soon put me at ease and when I left to go to Pawling I felt exactly as I did after my first interview with President Leigh, that all had gone well.

He asked me to call him when I returned from the Thomases, but I was not equal to hearing what I feared might be bad news. It was Lowell who telephoned and brought me word that the book had been accepted.

Cripple Creek Days, the story of "The Greatest Gold Mining Camp on Earth," where I had spent my girlhood, was published in the fall of 1958, a few months before my seventy-fifth birthday.